Cont<

List of tables and maps   11

Preface   13

PART 1   THE PROCESS

1   A new life overseas?   15

    Emigrants past and present   16
    Why emigrate?   17
    Putting migration into perspective   18
    Are you a model migrant?   19

2   The immigration hurdle   21

    Different countries, different approaches   22
    Relations have their uses   23
    How the selection system works   24
    How to apply   26
    Where to seek outside help   27
    Must you use a migration consultant?   28
    How to choose a migration consultant   29
    How to become a citizen   30

3   Putting yourself in the picture   31

    Using libraries and bookshops   31
    Periodicals for would-be migrants   33
    High commissions, embassies, consulates and
      state offices   34
    Tourist boards and chambers of commerce   34
    Where to obtain briefing notes   35
    Attending seminars and open days   36
    Visiting the country   36
    How to make use of contacts abroad   37

4 Weighing up the pros and cons 41

Counting the cost 41
What benefits do you expect? 42
Will you gain a better standard of living? 42
Will you gain a better future for the family? 43
Will you find a more egalitarian society? 45
Will you find a better environment? 45
Will you gain better business or work prospects? 50
Should you aim for employment or self-employment? 50
Are you suited to be an emigrant? 51
Which country should you opt for? 54
Which region offers the best prospects? 54

5 How to find a job 57

How to search for a job from the UK 58
Job search visits 62
Business visits 63
Delaying the job search 64

6 Preparing for the move 65

Arranging your arrival 65
Banking 66
Briefings 66
Cancellations and disconnections 68
Car 68
Children 69
Clothing 70
Driving licence 71
Electoral registration 71
Financial advice 71
Forwarding of mail 72
Your home in the UK 72
Insurance 73
Investments 74
Legal matters 75
Medical matters 75
National Insurance 77
Passport and visa 77
Pensions 78
Pets 79
Power of attorney 80
Removals 80
Taxation 82

Contents

Travel arrangements 83
Your will 83
Making a checklist 83

7 Settling in successfully 85

Accommodation 85
Banking 87
Customs 87
Driving 87
Finding work 88
Getting to know the people 89
Health care 89
Homesickness 90
Mailing address 90
Registration 91
Schooling 91
Starting work 91
Taxation 92
Utilities 92

PART 2 THE COUNTRIES

8 Australia 93

States 95
Territories 97
Living in Australia 97
Immigration prospects 98
Immigration checklist 99
The points test 101
The role of the sponsor 106
Driving 107
Education 107
Taxation 107
Social security 107
House purchase 109
Job-finding 109
Further information 109

9 Canada 111

The regions of Canada 113
Living in Canada 116
Immigration prospects 117

The immigration process   119
Business migration   122
Temporary visas   123
Education   123
Social security   125
House purchase   125
Job-finding   126
Migration consultants in the UK   126
Further information   126

10   New Zealand   129

The economy   130
North Island   130
South Island   131
Immigration prospects   131
Immigration checklist   132
Non-immigrants   134
Social security   135
Education   135
Job-finding   138
Immigration consultants   138
Housing and cars   138
Further information   139

11   South Africa   141

The political and historical background   141
The country   142
The people   143
Immigration policy   144
Immigration procedures   145
Citizenship   149
Financial considerations   149
Cost of living   150
Housing   150
Health and social security   150
Education   150
Migration consultants   152
Jobsearch   152
Settling in   152
Further information   153

12   United States of America   154

The regions of America   156

Immigration prospects 160
Immigration checklist 161
Prohibited immigrants 164
How to apply for an immigrant visa 164
Non-immigrant (temporary) visas 165
Other non-immigrant visas 171
Education 172
Social security 172
Taxation 173
Accommodation 173
Salaries 174
Housing costs 174
Job-finding 174
Migration consultants 174
Further information 174

13 Europe and the rest of the world 177

The European Union 179
Other European countries 180
The Middle East and North Africa 180
Africa 181
Asia 182
The Caribbean 182
Latin America 182

PART 3   THE ALTERNATIVES

14 Alternatives to emigration 183

Study abroad 183
Work experience 185
Contract work 186
An overseas posting with your firm 187
The world is your workplace 187

PART 4   REFERENCE

Appendix   Job search kit 189

Points to remember when submitting applications 189
Sample application letters 190
Sample CVs 192
How should you behave at an interview? 194

Further reading   195

    General   195
    Australia   197
    Canada   198
    New Zealand   199
    South Africa   200
    United States   200
    Europe   201
    Other countries   202

UK directory   203

    General   203
    Education   204
    Financial planning   205
    Government departments   206
    Insurance and pensions   206
    Migration services   207
    Other consultants   208
    Removal firms   208

Country directory   211

    Australia   211
    Canada   212
    New Zealand   215
    South Africa   216
    United States of America   218

Index   221

List of Tables & Maps

1	Shopping list	38
2	Indicators of standards of living	44
3	Rainfall chart	46
4	Temperature chart	48
5	Chart to test your expectations and requirements	55
6	Checklist: things to do before leaving	84
7	Map of Australia	94
8	Points table for emigration to Australia	102
9	Business skills test for emigration to Australia	104
10	Projected house prices in Australia, 1994-6	108
11	Average salaries in Australia, 1991	108
12	Most liveable and comfortable city in Australia, 1993	108
13	Map of Canada	112
14	Points system for emigration to Canada	118
15	Informal assessment form for emigration to Canada	120
16	Average house prices in Canada, 1993, going from west to east	124
17	Map of New Zealand	128
18	Self-assessment form for emigration to New Zealand	136
19	Map of South Africa	140
20	Preliminary immigration questionnaire for South Africa	146

11

21 Sample house prices, 1993, South Africa   151

22 Map of USA   154

23 US non-immigrant visa application form   166

24 US extension/change of status form   168

25 Typical starting salaries for new graduates in the USA 174

26 USA regional house price trends   175

27 USA average earnings by occupation and sex   176

28 Map of southern Europe and the Mediterranean   178

29 Reply to a job advertisement   190

30 Speculative application letter   191

31 Curriculum Vitae (résumé)   192

32 Alternative to a CV   193

Preface

For centuries people have been leaving their countries in search of a better life elsewhere and the tradition lives on. A survey conducted in 1993 revealed that half the population of the UK would like to go and live abroad. Yet for every thousand who express such an interest, only a handful actually succeed in their aim, and of that handful there may be one or two who discover they have chosen unwisely.

This book is designed to assist you as would-be-emigrants to make the right choice and to advise you on how to set about this major step. It has never been more essential to have such information at your fingertips, for although Australia, Canada, New Zealand, South Africa and the United States of America continue to attract migrants in large numbers, they no longer have an open-door policy on immigration. There is no point in building up your hopes of starting a new life unless you stand a good chance of getting in.

The book is essentially a starting point which will, it is hoped, prompt you to think seriously about your aims and discover the best way to achieve them. For ease of reference the addresses of organisations mentioned in this book are listed in the directories at the end.

Although the information is as up-to-date as possible, countries review their immigration policies from time to time and modify their regulations in the light of their findings. Another problem is that fluctuating exchange rates make cost of living comparisons difficult. Furthermore, because of the effect of world recession on individual economies, it is difficult to predict with any certainty which places will offer the best job or business opportunities to a newcomer in the future.

This book could not have been written without help and suggestions from a number of people, including staff at embassies, high commissions and migration consultancies. I am particularly grateful to the following people who have given generously of their time to answer my questions or check my facts: Sanwar Ali of BCL Immigration Services; Robert Hall of Carriere Hall and Associates; Grahame Igglesden of Australian

Immigration Services; Ira Levy of US Visa Consultants; Brian Palmer of Network Migration Services; John Reeves of SA Placements; Jennifer Choudhuri, Stuart McMinn, Helen Norman, Richard Starks, David Watson and others.

Constructive comments and information that could be included in future editions of this book are welcome; you can contact me c/o How To Books Ltd. For those of you contemplating a new life abroad, may I wish you every success.

Roger Jones

1
A New Life Overseas

'Mr Micawber, I wonder you have never turned your thoughts to emigration.'

'Madam,' returned Mr Micawber, 'it was the dream of my youth and the fallacious aspiration of my riper years.' I am thoroughly persuaded, by the by, that he had never thought of it in his life.

(Charles Dickens: David Copperfield)

If, unlike Mr Micawber, you have 'turned your thoughts' to emigration, this book is for you. You may have already thought hard and long about the attractions of moving to another country, or may just be in the preliminary stages wondering whether it is an idea worth pursuing.

'Emigration' means moving to another country with a view to settling down there permanently, which is quite different from going off to live in another country for a few months or a couple of years. In that case the commitment is essentially short-term, and you have a home-base to return to. If, on the other hand, you decide to emigrate, you will be uprooting yourself completely and, in effect, embarking on a new life.

Emigration is a long-term commitment, so it is essential to research all its implications thoroughly before coming to a firm decision. It is just not possible to decide to emigrate to Australia one day and be there the following week. Even if you are simply planning to take up a short-term contract and have no plans to stay, such a time-scale would be almost impossible. The processing of immigrants for countries such as New Zealand, the USA and Canada takes time.

Why? Because it is not so much a case of your choosing your country of residence, but of the country's choosing you. You would not invite someone to live in your house for the rest of your life unless you knew quite a lot about them — whether he or she is of good character, self-supporting and in good health, for example. In the same way the governments of countries that take in migrants are equally selective.

They can afford to be. One migration consultancy specialising in New

15

Zealand receives between 1,000 and 1,500 enquiries about migration each week. Yet New Zealand is not so desperately short of people that its government needs to attract such large numbers. On the contrary, its government now imposes a worldwide quota on settlers (currently 25,000) representing the number of people it feels it can absorb into the economy in a single year. The same is true of other English-speaking countries dealt with in this book.

EMIGRANTS PAST AND PRESENT

Things were different in Victorian times and before. The main countries mentioned in this book were once British colonies which needed settlers to populate the wide-open spaces and develop the economy. Even when these countries became fully independent, British migrants were still generally sought out in large numbers. Indeed, Australia, New Zealand and South Africa continued to offer assisted passages well after the end of the Second World War.

Some of the early migrants left the British Isles out of necessity rather than by choice. Lack of religious freedom at home prompted groups of English Puritans to sail off to found colonies in Massachusetts based on their religious ideals, and they were soon followed by Roman Catholics (to Maryland) and Quakers (to Pennsylvania).

Others left for economic reasons — because their prospects of making a living at home were extremely poor. Some went willingly, while others had to be persuaded. A striking incidence of this was the Irish potato famine in the mid-nineteenth century, when millions left that country to seek a new life elsewhere. More often than not they were encouraged to leave ('shovelled out') by their landlords who would otherwise have had to support them out of the parish rate.

A third type of migrant was given no choice at all. British criminals were shipped off to the other side of the world — from which the authorities hoped they would never return. Eventually, anti-transportation leagues were founded on that continent which called for an end to this policy, and the last convict ship docked at Freemantle, Western Australia in 1868.

Today, the situation is quite different. A person with even a short criminal record is likely to have his or her application turned down by the immigration service of any of the countries in this book. Nor is a person who is able-bodied but without formal qualifications likely to fare much better — unless he or she has very close relations who are already resident in the country in question. Countries are now restricting the quantity of migrants they take in and paying more heed to the quality of each applicant. Emigration is no longer an option for everybody.

In the past thousands of people sailed over the oceans in a state of ignorance: their ideas of what life would be like in their adoptive homelands were based on the reports (often extravagant, usually misleading) of people who had already made the journey. Reality did not always coincide with the dream. 'Now, Father, I think this is the Promised Land, but there are faults in it,' wrote one emigrant to Australia in 1848 to his family back home. [1]

Today's emigrants have many advantages over their predecessors. Thanks to developments in communication you can find out all you need to know about a place before you take the plunge. If you prefer to see for yourself rather than rely on the (often coloured) opinions of others, you can pay a brief visit to the country before you make up your mind.

WHY EMIGRATE?

Although many emigrants in the past were driven to settle abroad because of starvation, poor conditions, lack of work or religious persecution, others set sail because they were attracted to the opportunities presented by life in a foreign land. They felt they could carve out a better life for themselves and their families.

'Are the circumstances of the country such that a man of Mr Micawber's abilities would have a fair chance of rising in the social scale?' Mrs Micawber injects a sensible, positive note into the question of emigration. There is little point in venturing abroad unless there are reasonable prospects.

At this point it is worth considering some of the reasons why emigration may appeal to you.

● poor economic prospects at home
● the high cost of living
● a polluted, congested environment
● disillusionment with the political situation
● dissatisfaction with the climate
● a desire to escape from personal problems
● a restricted lifestyle.

These are so-called 'push factors' — conditions which prompt people to consider change. But there are also some positive factors to bear in mind:

- a chance to join close friends and relatives
- better economic prospects
- a better quality of life
- new challenges
- a cleaner environment
- a more egalitarian society
- a better future for your children.

These are sometimes called 'pull factors' — the things that attract would-be emigrants.

PUTTING MIGRATION INTO PERSPECTIVE

Most of us suffer at times from the delusion that the grass is greener on the other side of the hill. Perhaps it is, but very often our perceptions are based on insufficient or inaccurate information. The grass may be greener because the rainfall is heavier; the advantages are usually counterbalanced by drawbacks.

When the economy is in a depressed state or the national sports teams lose match after match, national morale drops and people are apt to assume that prospects elsewhere are rosier, even if they are not. The truth is we are living in a global economy these days where no country is immune from economic swings. If your prospects look bleak in this country, are you absolutely sure that you would fare better elsewhere?

Andrew Carnegie migrated from the UK to the United States where he founded a steel empire and amassed a considerable fortune. Yet it was not the country that brought him success, but his own personal qualities. 'The only encouragements we hold out to strangers are — a good climate, fertile soil, wholesome air and water, plenty of provisions, good pay for labour, kind neighbors, good laws, a free government, and a hearty welcome,' observed Benjamin Franklin. [2]

Let us look at this another way. Migration is not a one-way phenomenon. Australians such as Clive James and Rolf Harris, New Zealanders such as Des Wilson and Kiri Te Kanawa, and South Africans such as Janet Suzman and Anthony Sher have found greater opportunity in the UK than in their own countries. Countless refugees from Eastern Europe, East Africa and Asia have arrived here penniless and built up thriving businesses.

A change of scene may well act as a stimulus, but you should not assume that your fortunes will revive the moment you set foot in a new country. The rosy-coloured view of the United States as sometimes

depicted in Hollywood movies masks the fact that poverty and disillusionment exist across the Atlantic, too. A traffic jam is a traffic jam wherever
you happen to be, and you should not assume that everything you see in
films and soap operas accords with reality.

If you are emigrating for purely negative reasons (i.e. you are pushed
into emigration) you should think again. Foreign places are not ideal
venues for solving personal problems and if you are unable to make a go
of your life in Britain, there is no guarantee that you will fare better
elsewhere. Another consideration is that immigration officers are looking
for people who are positive about their target country and also have
something useful to offer.

ARE YOU A MODEL MIGRANT?

Migration often turns out to be a selection process. Countries are looking
for people who can contribute to their economic development. For this
reason some countries are now reviewing their policy of admitting retired
immigrants, especially since the proportion of pensioners in their populations is rising dramatically.

What sort of people are they looking for? If you have a majority of the
following you are off to an excellent start:

- good employment prospects
- good qualifications
- funds to tide you over until you find a job
- friends or relatives who will help you settle in
- some experience of the country concerned
- good health
- good character (i.e. no criminal record)
- a job offer or substantial investment funds.

Yet a good score on the above list is not enough to guarantee success
in another country. Not all wines travel well and the same holds true of
people. Venturing to a new country calls for a change of outlook and
perhaps a change in temperament too.

Look at the following list of adjectives.

adaptable
resourceful
tactful
communicative

determined
innovative
balanced
tolerant (openminded).

Ask yourself and your confidants how well these words describe you. If most of them do, then you would appear to have the qualities needed to settle down successfully in a different country. If not, you need to consider very carefully whether emigration is a suitable option for you.

This book is not intended to encourage people to emigrate in the style of the recruiting sergeant in days gone by. Rather it seeks to assist you to come to an informed decision as to whether this is the right step for you to take and suggest ways in which you can ensure that your migration plans proceed smoothly.

Notes
[1] Emigrant's letter, *Bradford Observer*, 7 December 1848.
[2] Benjamin Franklin, quoted in *Hints to Emigrants*, Liverpool, E. Rushton, 1817.

2
The Immigration Hurdle

The perceived need to control, direct or at least influence migration flows is by no means recent. (Philip Ogden) [1]

As we have seen, governments no longer fall over themselves to attract newcomers to their countries and assisted passages for immigrants are a thing of the past. Today the difficulty lies not so much in selecting a country to emigrate to but rather in obtaining approval to live and work there.

There is no point in building up your hopes — putting your own house on the market, giving in your notice, sending off to Adelaide, Auckland or Alberta for estate agents' brochures, scanning the classified job ads in overseas newspapers — if the authorities are likely to turn down your application. Your first course of action should be to find out whether you are likely to qualify for that important residence visa.

If you have very close relatives in the country concerned, you should not have too much difficulty in acquiring an immigrant visa, but you should not regard acceptance as either automatic or instantaneous. You could, for instance, be turned down on health grounds or because you fail to meet the character requirements.

For people who have no relations in the country it is qualifications and skills that count. Countries are looking for people who have some contribution to make to their societies, not hangers-on who will be a drain on the public purse. Nationality or the colour of one's skin are immaterial: these days multi-cultural immigration policies are in place virtually everywhere.

Moreover these policies are dynamic: the economic situation is in a constant state of flux and the policy has to be flexible enough to meet changing requirements. If the economy is booming there may well be a need for extra hands on deck to cope with the workload. On the other hand, if unemployment spirals upwards it is hard for the authorities to justify the importation of extra labour.

Although you may be convinced that you have a great deal to offer, it is the immigration officials who have the final say — although there are usually provisions for an appeal if you are turned down. Yet acceptance does not usually depend on the luck of the draw: there are usually guidelines set down, and knowledge of these will help you determine whether you are eligible or not.

DIFFERENT COUNTRIES, DIFFERENT APPROACHES

Today you cannot normally enter a country as a visitor and take up employment without securing a permit to do so. (The member states of the European Union are the exception.) Governments take a dim view of people who overstay their welcome or who are admitted as tourists but start working illegally, and they have powers to deport. In most cases you need to obtain your work visa before you leave.

The US has a complicated system of visas divided into two categories: permanent and temporary (non-immigrant). If you do not have close relations in the country or vast sums to invest, your best plan may well be to get a job and apply for a temporary (non-immigrant) visa, which can usually be extended. If you decide to take up permanent residence at some later date you can petition the authorities within the country for a change of status. There is, however, no guarantee that your petition will be approved.

Canada does not make such a rigid distinction between permanent and temporary visas, and you may well find it more beneficial to apply for a full immigrant visa at the outset. South Africa, New Zealand and Australia issue various types of visas. In all cases certain conditions have to be met.

Most immigration policies appear to fulfil three criteria:

- family reunion: to bring together close family members

- humanitarian: to offer asylum to refugees and displaced persons

- economic: to attract inward investors as well as people with much needed skills in order to improve commercial and technological competitiveness.

Governments are no longer interested in promoting immigration for the sole purpose of increasing the population, even though the population of some countries would decline without immigration. Even the family reunion category can no longer be regarded as sacrosanct, and in countries where unemployment is high a job offer or good qualifications may be required in addition to family ties.

Case study
NR and his fiancée decided to buy a house in Florida with the intention of getting married and settling down there. He achieved the first of his aims, but the second proved more complicated. The couple had entered the United States on visitor's visas which are valid for a limited period of time (normally six months) and do not entitle a person to stay in the country indefinitely.

He engaged a lawyer to obtain a so-called 'green card' for him which would allow him to have permanent resident status and also to work in the United States. He succeeded in extending his stay a further six months, and during this time he received a job offer which was conditional on his obtaining a work visa. However, his application for a 'green card' was turned down, his extension was over, and a year after his arrival in the US he put his house up for sale and returned home.

The moral of this story is that you should not assume that you are entitled to work or reside indefinitely in a foreign country. Many countries have clearly defined rules as to who qualifies for work visas or residence permits, and it is advisable to investigate these carefully before you make any financial commitments. Otherwise you may be disappointed.

RELATIONS HAVE THEIR USES

Family reunion cases are usually treated sympathetically, and a high proportion of migrants approved by the countries discussed in this book tend to be people with close relatives living there. For the USA, for instance, around 70 per cent of places are allocated to family-sponsored immigrants. South Africa is an exception to the rule.

The term 'close relatives' usually extends to spouses, children or parents — sometimes to brothers and sisters. Each country has its own rules, and you need to acquaint yourself with these.

If your fiancé(e) is a resident of the country in question (better still, a citizen) a permit is usually issued as a matter of course, and the same applies if you have an unmarried partner (subject to certain criteria being met). Marriages of convenience (where you marry someone merely to gain a residence visa) are frowned on and, if detected, will lead to the refusal of an application.

Even if you have uncles, aunts, cousins or friends living in a country who are prepared to sponsor you, this may turn out to be of minimal benefit when it comes to obtaining a visa, and you will probably have to submit an application as an independent immigrant. Yet the existence of family members in the country to which you wish to emigrate might well sway a decision in your favour, especially if you can call on their help to settle you in.

HOW THE SELECTION SYSTEM WORKS

Let us look at the immigration system in more detail.

What are immigration quotas?

Most countries now set annual numerical limits (or quotas) on the people they will accept as immigrants. Some categories may be exempt from these limits (notably close relations) and can be processed immediately in most cases. Migrants in other categories have to join a queuing system, so to speak, and when all the places allocated for the year are used up, those who fail to gain a place have to try their luck the following year.

Non-immigrant visas, by contrast, are not normally subject to numerical limitations. These are visas that allow you to stay in a particular country for a certain period, and may be tied to a particular appointment.

How the points system works

Australia, Canada and New Zealand have a points system for determining immigrant eligibility which works on a similar principle to that used by credit rating agencies in determining credit applications. In most cases details of the system in operation are published, and you can work out what your chances are of qualifying for an immigrant visa.

The system usually takes into account your age and level of qualification. The more points you get the better your prospects of being granted residence status. Often there is a pass mark; if you achieve this mark or better it, acceptance should be automatic — unless you are turned down on medical or security grounds. If you score below the pass mark — but not too far below — your application may be put in a pool, from which the better scoring applicants are drawn to make up their immigrant numbers.

You should note that marks can be raised or lowered in order to regulate the number of immigrant visas issued.

What are 'priority and approved occupations'?

Certain skills are in greater demand than others. If you are a paramedic, a computer scientist, or an electronics engineer you may find that yours is considered a priority occupation. Where a points system operates you may be accorded extra points.

In Canada, for instance, in 1993 you would be granted bonus points if you were a cook, a blacksmith, a machine repairer, a therapist or a dental hygienist. In 1994 these occupations may be discarded in favour of other categories: the priority occupation list is forever subject to change.

Australia has no priority occupations at present. New Zealand has a system of approved occupations, but this has diminished in significance since the high pass mark currently required virtually excludes people without post-school qualifications. The United States has certain employment categories for which approval is virtually automatic (e.g. nurses).

Which places are priority areas?
In some cases there may be an advantage if you aim to live away from the major conurbations or your sponsors do. In Australia certain regions are 'designated areas', and you may score extra points if you plan to live here. Currently New South Wales is not a designated area but South Australia is.

Countries are particularly keen to encourage investment in these areas, since investment normally creates extra jobs. Hence lower levels of investment may be accepted in priority areas from people who are keen to gain immigrant status.

How to gain recognition of qualifications and expertise
The fact that you have a degree or diploma does not automatically entitle you to practise your trade or profession in any country of the world. For instance, doctors and nurses who wish to work in the United States normally have to take an examination which measures their competence, and this holds true for other occupations as well.

When allocating points the Australian authorities will normally assess your qualifications and experience by Australian standards. For this reason it is important to have as much supporting evidence of your employment and education as possible, and to be prepared to supply additional information if the immigration officials require it.

It is worth while noting that in federal countries licensing procedures may vary from state to state. Thus in Canada, a teacher who is licensed to teach in Nova Scotia may not be eligible to teach in Saskatchewan. Clearly, it is essential to find out the procedures for having your qualifications recognised at an early stage in the emigration process.

Why you could be prohibited

Many countries set great store by applicants who are healthy and of good character. If you suffer from a communicable disease, mental instability and a host of other disabilities you risk being turned down. New Zealand, for instance, lays down very strict guidelines to its immigration officers on this matter, and you might be turned down on the grounds of being overweight!

Good character is also important. Although Australians express pride in having forbears who were in convict settlements, they are unlikely to look with favour on applications from ex-criminals. While they will overlook minor misdemeanours committed in the distant past, you may be required to sign a sworn affidavit to the effect that you have not committed any major crime. If you have lived abroad, you may have to produce a police certificate from the authorities there.

Political affiliation is another potential cause of trouble. While the United States is unlikely to turn you down on account of your membership of the Bagshot and District Green Party, if you have been a political agitator or a member of an extremist group, do not be surprised if your application is refused.

HOW TO APPLY

The time-lag between the filing of your application and actual acceptance can be considerable. You should therefore desist from winding up your affairs and announcing to the world and his wife that you plan to emigrate until written approval of your applications comes through. Bear in mind that no matter how good you feel your case to be, you could still be turned down.

The first step — after reading this book, of course — is to get in touch with the immigration division of the nearest embassy, consulate or high commission of the country to which you wish to emigrate, and ask for information on the procedures for obtaining an immigration visa.

If appropriate, you will then be sent an application form with instructions on how to fill it in. (In some cases this is preceded by a preliminary application form which offers an assessment of your likelihood of success: the Canadian High Commission in London offers this service free.) The main application form is normally extremely detailed and should be completed carefully.

When you send it off you will need to enclose a fee and supporting documentation. This might include:

- a birth certificate

- a medical report

- a marriage certificate (if applicable)

- a police certificate (if you have lived outside the UK in recent years)

- a CV

- testimonials from employers

- photographs

- photocopies of qualifications (possibly authenticated by a solicitor)

- evidence of family relations (for family-sponsored migrants)

- evidence of financial status (especially for business migrants).

While the initial vetting procedure might take a month, it can take much longer to process an application. Recent statistics from the Department of Immigration, Local Government and Ethnic Affairs in Australia indicate the average processing time for an independent visa is twelve months or more, while for a spouse it is five months.

You may well be called to the high commission or embassy for an interview with an immigration officer. Interviews of this nature can be quite probing. The officer has to be convinced that you are a bona fida emigrant and likely to be an asset to the country. But the occasion is also an opportunity for you to ask questions and clear up any doubts there may be in your mind.

The application process can be a protracted affair. You may be tempted to hurry things along by telephoning the embassy or high commission from time to time, but this may in fact be counter-productive and actually ___ ne processing time.

___ imes you have to rely on someone else to start the ball rolling. ___ ce, in the case of certain categories of migrants to the United ___ the sponsoring relative or prospective employer who has to file ___ ion.

___ O SEEK OUTSIDE HELP

___ immigration services are not generally in the business of

The Williams Family
12 Crofton Road
Ngaio
Wellington 6004

encouraging people to emigrate; their primary task is to screen applicants and turn down those who do not conform to the criteria laid down. However, they may be able to provide you with some written information.

Immigration clerks and officials deal with scores of applications a day and simply do not have the time to offer you advice on how to present your credentials successfully. If you fail to make out a good case for yourself by not submitting the relevant information, you have no-one to blame but yourself if your application is not accepted.

Because so much depends on getting your application right you may well consider enlisting the services of an immigration lawyer or a migration consultant, as many business investors do. If your case is complicated or stands on the borderline between acceptance and rejection it could be advantageous to have someone working for you who knows how to present you to the authorities in the best possible light. There will, however, be fees to pay.

Immigration lawyers are usually registered with the bar in their country as being able to undertake business of this nature. Immigration (or migration) consultants are often former immigration officials who know the ropes and have useful inside knowledge. Both can help prepare your application (or suggest ways in which it might be improved) and can, if required, take you through the whole process of obtaining the visa.

Unfortunately migration consultancy has spawned a number of black sheep. There are stories in circulation of immigration specialists who have raised unrealistic expectations and charged fat fees, but have failed to produce the necessary permits for their clients. Canada now has a professional association of immigration consultants to improve standards of integrity and competence in the profession (which is a welcome move), and all migration consultants operating within Australia have to be registered with the Federal Government's Migration Agents' Registration Board.

The names and addresses of some migration consultants practising in the UK are included in the reference section at the end of the book but this does not imply endorsement on the part of author or publisher.

MUST YOU USE A MIGRATION CONSULTANT?

It is not necessary to employ an intermediary, particularly if your case is a straightforward one or you have close relatives in the country concerned. For instance, if you are married to a citizen of the country, normally there should be little, if any, difficulty in obtaining full immigrant status. However, you should never take anything for granted, and you will have to go through the correct procedures like everybody else.

If you are an independent migrant (i.e. you are planning to emigrate on the basis of your qualifications and skills) the situation is different. Immigration officials have no time to help you fill in your application or assist you in other ways; their job is more akin to that of a judge and jury. So you may well feel you need someone to act on your behalf, especially if you have little idea of how the immigration process works.

If you have doubts, you can get a rough idea of whether you are eligible by a process of self-assessment. In the chapters on some countries I have provided a step-by-step guide to help you. Please note, however, that the rules are subject to change and for the latest information you should refer to the relevant diplomatic mission or migrant newspapers. Some embassies and high commissions provide their own self-assessment packs, while the Canadian High Commission in London currently offers a preliminary assessment free of charge.

HOW TO CHOOSE A MIGRATION CONSULTANT

If you decide to take professional counsel, you need to choose your adviser carefully. Obtain brochures from two or more firms, and when you feel you have found the right person arrange for a face-to-face meeting. For this reason if you are applying from the UK it makes sense to approach a consultant or lawyer who is based in the UK or who pays regular visits to this country.

- Ask for an initial assessment as to your chances of acceptance as an immigrant. You either stand a good chance of getting a visa or you don't; and a reputable consultant will not take you on as a client unless he is confident that you have a good case.

- Establish what services the consultancy can offer. Does the consultant just fill in or check the application and submit it, or is he able to take you through the immigration process step by step and make representations on your behalf?

- Find out the consultant's background, qualifications — and success rate. A legal qualification is not essential provided the person can point to several years' experience in the migration field.

- Ask for a rundown of costs you are likely to incur, including immigration service fees. Do not assume that you have to take all the services the consultancy offers, if not all of them are appropriate to your needs.
- Enquire about other services with which the consultant may be able to help you, such as assistance when you arrive. Some may be able to put you in touch with employers, employment agencies, insurance and financial advisers, removal firms, estate agents, travel agents.

HOW TO BECOME A CITIZEN

Applying for an immigrant visa should not be confused with applying for naturalisation. As an immigrant you are granted residential status in a particular country but retain your present current nationality.

This means that you do not have as many rights and privileges as a full citizen of the country concerned. You cannot stand for public office or become an MP, you cannot vote in major elections, and you may well find that certain government jobs are closed to you.

After you have been in a country for a certain period — three years in the case of Canada — you can apply to become a citizen (naturalisation). While countries welcome such a move, there is no obligation for you to do so. Those who become naturalised usually opt for dual nationality (i.e. citizenship of their country of origin and their adopted country) which means they are eligible to hold two passports.

Notes
[1] Philip Ogden, *Migration and Geographical Change*, Cambridge University Press, 1984.

3
Putting Yourself in the Picture

When I wish to be misinformed about a country I ask a man who has lived there thirty years. (Lord Palmerston).[1]

Emigration is a major step which carries a certain degree of risk and cost, and nobody should stumble into it blindly. Yet some people make a decision to emigrate on the basis of incorrect, inadequate, misleading or out-of-date information.

The images of a country as presented in the press, on television or in films may be completely at variance with reality. Only a small percentage of US residents drive a Cadillac or live in Malibu; relatively few South Africans are involved in riots; and the number of Canadians who are lumberjacks is extremely small. If you want to start off on the right foot, it is essential to be well informed.

As a prospective emigrant you need to be proactive in your search for information, which means asking relevant questions. 'Unfortunately, many get the wrong answers because they don't ask the right questions,' writes Ian Gale. 'And for many even asking the right questions is not enough   they ask the wrong people and get the wrong answers.' [2]

Surprisingly, the most misleading information often comes from friends or relatives of migrants, according to an Australian government report cited by Mr Gale. In their effort to persuade others to join them they may paint too rosy a picture, or else they want to show how successful they have been. You should always bear in mind that what is paradise to one person can be sheer hell for another.

All personal impressions therefore need to be taken with a pinch of salt and supplemented by information from a wide range of sources. There is a good deal of very sound information available: it is just a matter of knowing where to look for it. This chapter will help you track it down.

USING LIBRARIES AND BOOKSHOPS

There are a number of useful handbooks for would-be migrants about all

31

the countries dealt with in this book. They include the *How to Live and Work in . . .* series from How To Books, the *Long Stays in . . .* series from David & Charles, and the *Culture Shock* series from Kuperard/Times Editions. (See individual country bibliographies.)

If you cannot find the book you need on the shelves of your local bookshop, a bookseller will be only too happy to order a copy for you. There are also specialist bookshops that you could try, such as the Travellers' Bookshop off Charing Cross Road in London or the bookshop of the Centre for International Briefing at Farnham Castle which offers a mail-order service. Outbound Newspapers and Consyl Publishing can also supply books on countries dealt with by their newspapers.

Alternatively, you could try your local public library; the larger it is the better. Most public libraries in the UK classify books according to the Dewey Decimal System and the books you will be interested in would be coded as follows:

Australia: 919.4
Canada: 917.1
New Zealand: 919.31
South Africa: 916.8
United States: 917.3

You should make for the relevant section of your library to see what is available. If you find nothing there is no need to despair, for even the smallest library is able to obtain books for you through the national inter-library loans network, though you may be asked to pay a small fee. A number of useful books are listed in the Bibliography at the end of this book, but a librarian may be able to suggest other titles. The *British Books in Print* catalogue or microfiche should also unearth some useful works.

Finally, two caveats. Some of the books you will come across are intended for tourists, not people who are planning to spend their work-a-day lives in a particular country and the contents will reflect this intention. Even if you find a book relevant to your needs, make sure it is reasonably up-to-date. A work published in the 1960s or 1970s is unlikely to offer an accurate picture of life in the 1990s.

Once you get down to your job search in earnest you will need the services of a large reference library with a section containing overseas business and telephone directories. The Centre for International Briefing, for instance, has a library and resource centre covering most countries of the world. A charge is made for its use.

PERIODICALS FOR WOULD-BE MIGRANTS

To keep abreast of what is happening in the country you are interested in you need to read its own newspaper and magazine reports.

While most quality daily newspapers have extensive foreign news coverage, you may find it more beneficial to read publications written with prospective migrants in mind. I have tracked down no fewer than seven such journals, each of which concentrates on a particular country and provides the latest information on immigration regulations, house prices and salaries together with news reports, travel articles and location briefings.

They also carry advertisements for removal companies, immigration consultants, travel firms, banks and estate agents — the type of organisation you will need to get in touch with if you decide to go ahead. However, they do not normally contain advertisements for jobs.

The publishers are:

● Outbound Newspapers: *Australian News, Canada News, South Africa News, Going USA.* Outbound also operate a mail-order books service.

● Consyl Publishing: *Australian Outlook, New Zealand Outlook.* Consyl also acts as distributor for a number of Australian and New Zealand magazines and sells books by mail order.

● *New Zealand News UK.* This functions partly as a newspaper for New Zealanders in the UK, but also contains information of interest to migrants.

These newspapers, which are free, are not normally obtainable in newsagents, although Outbound distribute their publications through various travel agents, removal firms and diplomatic missions. The best idea is to contact the publisher of the title that interests you and take out a postal subscription. Charges are usually modest.

There are a number of other periodicals published in the UK which carry overseas job advertisements and the occasional article on emigration. They include:

● *Jobfinder* (Overseas Consultants)
● *Overseas Jobs Express* (Island Publishing)
● *Nexus* (Expat Network).

Addresses are given either in the Bibliography or the Directory at the end of this book.

HIGH COMMISSIONS, EMBASSIES, CONSULATES AND STATE OFFICES

If you decide to proceed further you would do well to seek information from the information officer or immigration officials at the diplomatic mission of the country of your choice. You can do this by phone, though sometimes — particularly in the case of the US Embassy — expect a long wait for your call to be answered. Better still — if they have a library or reading room you can use — visit the place. To use some facilities you may have to make a prior appointment.

In the case of both Canada and Australia you should not overlook the offices of the agents-general of the different states. Often the individual provinces or states seem keener on wooing potential migrants and investors than the federal governments, and can often provide you with up-to-date information on the job situation and economic climate as well as useful contacts (e.g. professional associations, chambers of commerce).

Their reading rooms often take the leading newspapers of the countries or states/provinces; and it would be worth your while to peruse the job columns to see what the jobs market is like. After all, there is little point in moving to a region of the country where there is no market for your skills. Business and trade periodicals are also worth looking at, as they can offer an insight into the economy and the prospects in your particular sector.

TOURIST BOARDS AND CHAMBERS OF COMMERCE

For further information about the country in which you are interested you could get in touch with the relevant national tourist board, which is bound to have an office in London. The office can provide you with maps and brochures of the different regions of the country, and may also be able to recommend tour operators.

However, tourist brochures do not always show a true picture, since their purpose is to promote tourism and tourist spots, not to provide an introduction to living in the country. When you emigrate you will not spend your time visiting one scenic delight after another. On the other hand, many brochures have lists of addresses (notably, accommodation, government and state offices, hospitals and car hire firms) which could prove useful to you in the future.

A few overseas chambers of commerce have offices and reference libraries in London and if you are thinking of making an investment or starting a business in the country concerned, these could be a useful source of information.

WHERE TO OBTAIN BRIEFING NOTES

At a later stage in your research, perhaps when you have made the decision to emigrate, you will need to investigate in greater detail the living conditions in the country. Embassies and high commissions sometimes have leaflets on living costs, customs regulations, house prices, etc. and may have substantial booklets, some of which are listed in the Bibliography. But if you are unable to obtain sufficient information (or would like a second opinion) you could contact one of the following organisations which publish briefing notes that are updated on a regular basis.

- Women's Corona Society, which publishes *Notes for Newcomers* — short booklets giving details of accommodation, education facilities, employment opportunities for spouses, prices, etc.

- Employment Conditions Abroad, which produces an *Outline for Expatriates* on about 75 different countries

- Expat Network, which is rapidly expanding its range of location reports written for the most part by its members

- Inside Tracks and Christians Abroad which publish location reports

- Walker and Walker whose *Emigration Packs* include cost of living comparisons and lists of employers and employment agencies.

Many overseas banks have representative offices in London and you could enquire whether they have any literature which would be of interest to a potential migrant. The Financial and Migrant Information Service of the Commonwealth Bank of Australia, for instance, does a useful *Cost of Living and Housing Survey* for that country.

ATTENDING SEMINARS AND OPEN DAYS

While written material is very useful, you can also benefit from a face-to-face briefing where you can get specific questions answered. A number of organisations offer prospective emigrants a chance to ask questions and meet people who will be able to assist them to emigrate. These are quite distinct from exhibitions organised by travel companies designed to stimulate tourism.

Among the organisations which currently offer such a service are:

● SA Placements which runs regular seminars for people considering a move to South Africa. A typical seminar will deal with job prospects, immigration procedures, financial matters, housing, removals, the political outlook, etc.

● Consyl Publishing: organises an information day on Australia and New Zealand two or three times a year. Participants have an opportunity to meet immigration officials, immigration and recruitment consultants, removal firms, financial experts, etc.

● Network Migration Services which offers three-hour seminars on New Zealand at various locations throughout the UK, usually in the evening.

● BCL Immigration Services which runs one-day seminars on migration to the USA and Canada.

Other organisations may hold seminars from time to time, and will normally advertise the event in the national or local press or in one of the migrant newspapers listed above.

At a later stage when you are actually preparing to leave you may find it beneficial to have a briefing with Women's Corona Society (Corona International), Employment Conditions Abroad or the Centre for International Briefing (see Chapter 6), particularly if you have a prospective employer who is prepared to contribute to the cost. Some banks also offer briefings to migrants before departure.

VISITING THE COUNTRY

You have probably heard the story of the man who set his heart on emigration to New Zealand and eventually sold up and sallied forth to achieve his dream. Yet not long after his departure from this country he was back. It transpired that the country had not measured up to his expectations, and he found he could not stand the place.

His unfortunate experience illustrates the dangers of relying wholly on one's own instincts and the impressions of others. Once you have an inkling of the place you would like to emigrate to it makes sense to experience the country at first hand, if you have not already done so.

However, you need to ensure that your visit does not turn out to be a glorified holiday when in fact you should be aiming for a reconnaissance. Your task must be to investigate the living conditions together with the work and business prospects; in which case sightseeing and entertainment will come near the bottom of your list of priorities.

True, visits to supermarkets, furniture and household equipment stores, and estate agents may sound mundane compared with river cruises and scenic coach tours, but they will offer a better insight into the life that awaits you. To get off to a good start you might make out a shopping list — on the lines of the one suggested in Fig. 1 — and price the different goods on it.

A number of organisations offer special migrant information tours which offer people contemplating migration a taste of what to expect. The South Australian Government Immigration Unit has organised visits of this nature in cooperation with *Australian News*, while Network Migration Services offers a *Seeing is Believing Tour* to New Zealand. Other tours especially for migrants are advertised from time to time in the migrant newspapers.

There are other travel companies which will meet you on arrival, arrange short-stay accommodation and organise an itinerary. Several of them advertise in the migrant newspapers mentioned earlier.

HOW TO MAKE USE OF CONTACTS ABROAD

I have left friends and relations until last, partly because they are the most obvious source of information, but mainly because they can be the most misleading. There is a risk that they may tell you what you want to know (the good things), not what you ought to know (the drawbacks).

If you have gathered information diligently from some of the sources suggested above you will have a clearer idea of how they can help you. For example, they may be able to provide you with an idea of the cost of living by sending you a list of prices.

This need not be an imposition. Many supermarkets these days provide itemised bills, and a few of these will give you a very good idea of how

Shopping list

(Quote either price or price range — as appropriate)

Furniture

3 piece lounge suite
dining table with 6 chairs
sideboard/buffet

double bed (incl. mattress)
single bed (incl. mattress)
wardrobe (in some countries fitted
wardrobes are the norm)

Electrical goods

fridge/freezer 400 litres
washing machine (standard size)
microwave oven
electric stove
iron
kettle/jug

vacuum cleaner
portable radio
TV set (48 cm)
video recorder
hi-fi (turntable, radio, CD player,
cassette, speakers)

Household items

crockery set (36 piece china)
crockery set (36 piece earthenware)
cutlery (44 piece, stainless steel)
pans (3 saucepans and frying pan)
bathtowel

handtowel
sheets (pair)
blanket
duvet
washing detergent 500 gm

Transport and communication

(in the case of vehicles include
new and used prices)
supermini (e.g. Ford Fiesta)
family car (e.g. Vauxhall Astra)
executive car (Volvo 740)
motor cycle 500 cc
bicycle
airfare (1,000 miles)

train fare (100 miles)
bus fare (50 miles)
local phone call (5 minutes)
international phone call (5
minutes)
driving licence
typical car insurance for person of
your age

Fig. 1. Shopping list.

Shopping list continued

Clothes

Women

skirt
long sleeved dress
cardigan
shoes

Men

suit
sports jacket/blazer
trousers
shirt
shoes

Food and drink

breakfast cereal (e.g. cornflakes)
    500 gm
beef 1 kg
butter/margarine 250 gm
cheese (cheddar type) 500 gm/1 lb
chicken 1 kg
coffee instant (e.g. Nescafé)
    200 gm
eggs medium 1 doz
fish (white) 500 gm/1 lb

flour (self-raising) 1 kg/2 lb
milk 1 litre
loaf large sliced white
milk 1 litre
peas frozen 500 gm
potatoes 1 kg/2 lb
sausages 1 kg
sugar granulated 2 kg
teabags 160 pack
tomatoes 500 gm/1 lb

Other

Add other items which you wish to include on the list

Fig. 1. Continued.

much your weekly grocery bill will come to. Many electrical and DIY stores publish price lists, and there are mail order firms that produce detailed shopping catalogues. See if they could send you copies of these, or else give you the addresses of the firms for you to contact.

Notes

[1] Lord Palmerston quoted in A.P. Thornton *The Imperial Idea and its Enemies* (1959).

[2] Ian Gale, *Successful Migrating to Australia*, Macdonald/Queen Anne Press, 1990.

HOW TO MASTER LANGUAGES

Roger Jones

With the expansion of international travel and the advent of the global market, languages are more valuable that ever before. Written for business people, students and others, this book discusses: why learn a language, which language to choose, language training and where to find it, getting down to language learning, children and languages, and language training in organisations. A huge reference section completes the book, giving information on an enormous variety of courses, guides and study material, providing an overview of the world's myriad languages and their use today. Roger Jones DipTESL is himself an experienced linguist, writer and educational consultant.

£8.99, 160pp illust. 1 85703 0923

Please add postage & packing (UK 1.00 per copy. Europe £2.00 per copy. World £3.00 per copy airmail).

How To Books Ltd, Plymbridge House, Estover Road, Plymouth PL6 7PZ, United Kingdom. Tel: (0752) 695745. Fax: (0752) 695699. Telex: 45635.

Credit card orders may be faxed or phoned.

4
Weighing Up the Pros and Cons

All our final decisions are made in a state of mind that is not going to last.
(Marcel Proust)

At this stage you should have some idea as to which country or countries you would like to emigrate to and whether you stand a chance of being accepted as an immigrant by any of them.

However, there is more to emigration than just cutting your way through the red tape. The absence of any bureaucratic obstacles is obviously welcome, but there are also other considerations:

- How much is it going to cost to move?
- What benefits do I expect to gain?
- Should I find a job or work for myself?
- Have I got what it takes to be a successful migrant?

Let us explore these points in depth.

COUNTING THE COST

Unless you have fixed yourself up with an indulgent employer who is prepared to foot the bill for your move, emigrating to another part of the world can turn out to be a costly business, particularly if you have dependants and a home. Among the major expenses you will incur are:

- immigration fees: these will normally set you back several hundred pounds

- fares: while it is reasonably cheap to fly to North America, fares — even discounted ones – to the Southern Hemisphere are expensive

- removal expenses: if you plan to ship a large number of household items to your new home you are talking of costs running into thousands of pounds

- temporary accommodation: the chances are that you will need to move into temporary accommodation — perhaps before you go, almost certainly on arrival — and short-term accommodation can be expensive; a substantial deposit may be payable

- additional living costs: these might include eating out, deposits for telephone and electricity connections, kitting out your new home.

If you have capital tied up in a house in this country you may well plan to realise your assets by selling it. However, it is unwise to count your chickens before they hatch; in recent years people have experienced difficulty selling up because the house market was flat. This has caused problems with immigration departments which expect you to use your visa within a certain period of the date of issue.

Bear in mind also that if you have not already fixed yourself up with a job on arrival you will need sufficient money to live on until you start earning your living. Not every country offers unemployment benefit to newcomers, and supplementary benefits as they exist in the UK may be practically unknown. To emigrate successfully you need some capital to tide you over the first few months.

WHAT BENEFITS DO YOU EXPECT?

There is little point in moving across the globe unless there are benefits to be gained at the end of the exercise. In Chapter 1 some of the reasons people give for emigrating were outlined. This is the time to do some soul-searching: What precisely do you hope to gain by the move?

- a better standard of living?
- a better future for my family?
- a more egalitarian society?
- a better environment?
- greater business or work opportunities?

Then ask yourself whether you think you will achieve these goals by migrating.

WILL YOU GAIN A BETTER STANDARD OF LIVING?

Some people move overseas in the expectation of earning higher salaries. However, you may well find that the cost of living is higher and there is little if any financial advantage. A better idea is to disregard the rate of exchange and look at the buying power of the money you will have at your disposal.

In some countries you may find that cars and consumer goods are more expensive than in the UK, in others less so. Some of the perks you received in the UK may be unknown overseas. Taxes could be higher and there may be extra expenses that you have not reckoned on, such as healthcare and higher fuel bills (for air-conditioning in hotspots, for extra heating in places like Canada). While a shopping list of comparative prices can be used as a guide it does not tell the whole story (see Chapter 3).

Bear in mind that housing costs may vary considerably according to the region of the country you are making for. In the USA, for example, buying or renting a house in California could cost you four times as much as in Oklahoma. Fig. 2 indicates how your standard of living would compare from country to country. (South Africa is omitted since direct comparisons are misleading.)

WILL YOU GAIN A BETTER FUTURE FOR THE FAMILY?

If you have a family you need to take their needs into consideration. What may be exciting and challenging for some people might turn out to be traumatic for their dependants. If your family have strong roots in the local community they might not relish the idea of moving.

The interests of your children (if you have any) have to be considered very carefully. It is not enough for them to have more space to play around in. The job markets of tomorrow will only have room for skilled and educated people so their education will have to be a priority. Where your children are making excellent progress at school, the last thing you want to do is disrupt their schooling. Their education may be at a crucial stage with important examinations looming, in which case you may well decide to defer you plans to emigrate.

On the other hand you may feel that the British educational system has its limitations and that the type of education obtainable overseas will be superior. It is difficult to come to any meaningful conclusions on this topic. Certainly schools (both state-run and private) in Australia, Canada and New Zealand (which for the most part follow a British-style education pattern) reach standards which are comparable with their counterparts in Britain, and may well be better resourced. Education in the United States is organised along different lines and standards tend to vary between school districts.

Item	Unit	Year	New Zealand	United States	Canada	Australia	United Kingdom
Area	sq. km (000)	1990	270.5§	9 372.6	9 976.1	7 686.8	244.8
Population	million	1990	3.4	251.5	26.6	17.1	57.4
Density	persons per sq. km	1990	12.6	26.8	2.7	2.2	234.5
Vital statistics							
Infant mortality rate	per 1000 live births	1990	8.3	9.2	7.2§	8.2	7.9
Life expectancy at birth male		1990	71.9	72.1	73.0*	73.9	72.8§
female		1990	78.0	79.0	79.7*	80.0	78.4§
Gross Domestic Product	$US billion at current prices and exchange rates	1991	41.5	5 552.2	595.9	295.5	1,008.8
GDP per capita	$US at current prices and exchange rates	1990	12,656	21,449	21,418	17,282	16,985
Average annual volume change	%	1980–90	1.9	2.9	2.9	3.2	2.6
Employment by sector							
Agriculture	%	1990	10.6	2.8	4.2	5.6	2.1
Industry	%	1990	24.6	26.2	24.6	25.4	29.0
Services	%	1990	64.8	70.9	71.2	69.0	68.9
Wages and prices							
Wages	average annual percent increase over five years to 1988	1988	8.9	2.8	3.8	5.3	8.4
prices		1988	11.3	3.5	4.2	7.1	4.7
Energy							
Total final energy consumption	tonnes of oil equivalent (million)	1990	9.8	1 373.9	158.9	58.7	147.0
Total production	tonnes of oil equivalent (million)	1990	11.5	1 630.8	274.8	158.4	205.3
External trade							
Imports (c.i.f.)	$US billion at current prices and exchange rates	1990	12.9	608.3	143.0	52.0	262.7
Exports (f.o.b.)	$US billion at current prices and exchange rates	1990	12.2	528.4	144.8	48.9	239.6
Sectoral contributions							
Agriculture	% of GDP	1989	8.6	2.0†	2.9†	4.1§	1.3‡
Industry	% of GDP	1989	26.7	29.2†	30.0†	31.0	30.0‡
Services	% of GDP	1989	64.7	68.8†	67.1†	65.0	68.7‡
Health and education							
Doctors	per 1000 of mean population	1990	1.9§	2.3	2.2		1.4§
Expenditure on health	% of GDP	1990	7.4	12.4	9.0	7.7	6.2
Expenditure on public education	% of GDP	1988–89	5.4	4.8‖	6.8	4.7‖	4.8
Television sets in use	per 1000 inhabitants	1986	358†	813	546†	472	534
Passenger cars	per 1000 inhabitants	1989	549	748	613	570	449
Consumers Price Index	% change from previous year	1991	2.6	4.2	5.6	3.2	5.8
Currency (exchange rate)	equivalent to $NZ1 mid-rate as at 1 Dec 1992	1992	1.00	0.52	0.66	0.76	0.34

*1986　　†1987　　‡1988　　§1989　　‖1986–87.

Sources: OECD Economic Survey of New Zealand, 1990, OECD in Figure 1992; World Statistics in Brief (UN Statistical Pocketbook) 1992.

Fig. 2. Indicators of standards of living.

44

WILL YOU FIND A MORE EGALITARIAN SOCIETY?

You may feel that your own society is irredeemably class-ridden and that you would fare better in a country where people are valued for their abilities rather than for their social status or title. Countries, such as Australia and the United States, set great store by the fact that everybody has the same rights and opportunities.

However things are not always what they seem, and if you scratch below the surface of your adopted country you will find a pecking order of sorts. Although Australians like to put their leaders in their place, there is no doubt about it that attending a prestigious private school will give your career a significant boost. And you will find considerable social stratification in parts of the United States: in Boston, for instance,

> . . . where the Lowells talk to the Cabots
> And the Cabots talk only to God. [1]

Not that this need bother you. A move to a foreign clime may have a liberating effect on your own attitudes. You are turning your back on your social origins and starting afresh.

WILL YOU FIND A BETTER ENVIRONMENT?

People who are used to working in London or other big cities are often keen to get away into less crowded surroundings. However, you could jump out of the frying pan into the fire: working in New York, Sydney or Toronto could prove just as stressful as working in London or Manchester with long journeys to work every day.

There is no disputing that all the countries treated at length in this book have plenty of wide open spaces, and those in the southern hemisphere, at least, boast a clean environment — outside the major cities at any rate. As for the weather you can expect, you should ignore the enticing pictures of blue skies and green fields that you see in the tourist brochures and pay heed to the rainfall and temperature tables in this chapter (Figs 3 and 4).

Whether the social environment represents an improvement as well is debatable. Crime is on the increase in most countries; you may find that the locals are cold and unfriendly; and if you are used to the cultural sophistication of London or Edinburgh, you may find Canberra or Cape Town somewhat provincial.

	Jan.	Feb.	Mar.	Apr.	May	June
UK						
London	54	40	37	37	46	45
Edinburgh	57	39	39	39	54	47
Australia						
Adelaide	20	18	25	46	67	76
Alice Springs	43	33	28	10	15	13
Brisbane	163	160	145	94	71	66
Canberra	46	43	56	41	46	56
Hobart	48	38	46	48	46	56
Perth	8	10	20	43	130	180
Sydney	89	102	127	135	127	117
Canada						
Edmonton	24	22	20	26	42	77
Halifax	140	119	113	113	108	94
Montreal	87	76	86	83	81	91
Toronto	66	58	66	66	71	63
Vancouver	214	161	151	90	69	65
New Zealand						
Auckland	79	94	81	97	127	137
Christchurch	59	43	48	48	66	66
South Africa						
Cape Town	17	13	24	60	97	105
Johannesburg	112	97	75	61	22	9
USA						
Anchorage	20	23	18	18	15	28
Chicago	41	33	66	94	81	110
Denver	13	18	31	46	64	41
Houston	81	84	69	107	119	107
Los Angeles	94	76	60	31	6	0
Miami	51	48	58	99	163	188
New York	81	79	107	97	97	81
St Louis	43	54	84	91	89	94
Seattle	153	107	91	61	41	36

Fig. 3. Rainfall chart (average monthly precipitation in millimetres).

	July	Aug.	Sep.	Oct.	Nov.	Dec.
UK						
London	57	59	49	57	64	48
Edinburgh	83	77	57	65	62	57
Australia						
Adelaide	66	66	53	43	28	25
Alice Springs	8	8	8	18	30	38
Brisbane	56	48	48	64	94	127
Canberra	46	56	41	56	48	51
Hobart	53	48	53	58	61	53
Perth	170	145	86	56	20	13
Sydney	117	76	74	71	74	74
Canada						
Edmonton	82	70	34	21	20	22
Halifax	94	95	117	120	143	132
Montreal	98	87	96	84	89	89
Toronto	74	61	66	58	63	61
Vancouver	39	44	83	172	198	243
New Zealand						
Auckland	145	117	107	107	89	79
Christchurch	69	48	46	43	48	59
South Africa						
Cape Town	98	83	49	52	36	25
Johannesburg	8	5	25	69	116	111
USA						
Anchorage	51	53	64	43	28	28
Chicago	91	89	86	58	53	53
Denver	48	38	31	25	20	15
Houston	84	94	124	94	86	94
Los Angeles	0	3	8	5	48	51
Miami	170	178	214	208	71	43
New York	97	102	94	86	104	97
St Louis	91	66	69	58	64	56
Seattle	18	33	51	86	143	160

Fig. 3. Continued.

	Jan.		Feb.		Mar.		Apr.		May	
UK										
London	5.5	1.1	6.0	1.1	8.8	2.3	10.8	4.0	13.5	6.3
Edinburgh	6.3	2.2	6.9	2.2	10.1	3.3	13.3	5.5	16.7	8.2
Australia										
Adelaide	30.0	10.5	30.0	16.7	27.2	15.0	22.8	12.8	18.9	10.0
Alice Springs	36.1	21.6	35.0	20.5	32.2	17.2	27.2	12.2	22.8	7.8
Brisbane	29.4	20.5	29.4	20.0	27.9	13.3	26.1	16.1	23.3	13.3
Canberra	27.8	12.8	27.8	12.8	24.4	10.5	19.4	6.7	15.5	2.8
Hobart	21.6	11.7	21.6	11.7	20.0	10.5	17.2	8.9	14.4	6.7
Perth	29.4	17.2	29.4	17.2	27.2	16.1	25.5	13.9	20.5	11.7
Sydney	25.5	18.3	25.5	18.3	24.4	17.2	21.6	14.4	18.9	11.1
Canada										
Edmonton	-8.6	-18.7	-6.8	-16.8	-0.3	-10.3	9.9	-1.8	17.1	4.4
Halifax	0.3	-7.2	0.7	-7.0	3.7	-3.6	8.9	0.9	14.4	5.4
Montreal	-5.5	-13.2	-3.8	-11.3	1.8	-5.3	10.6	2.3	18.3	8.6
Toronto	-0.8	-7.7	-0.1	-6.9	3.9	-3.2	11.8	3.3	18.2	8.6
Vancouver	5.6	0.0	7.2	1.1	10.0	2.8	13.9	5.0	17.2	8.3
New Zealand										
Auckland	22.8	15.5	22.8	15.5	21.6	15.0	19.4	13.3	16.7	10.5
Christchurch	21.1	11.7	20.5	11.7	18.9	10.0	16.7	7.2	13.3	15.5
South Africa										
Cape Town	26.4	16.7	26.6	16.5	25.8	15.6	22.6	13.3	19.7	11.0
Johannesburg	25.3	14.2	25.0	14.1	23.9	12.8	21.0	10.2	18.5	7.2
USA										
Anchorage	-6.2	-14.7	-3.0	-12.3	0.5	-10.1	6.9	-2.8	12.7	2.7
Chicago	0.6	-7.2	1.5	-6.3	6.4	-1.7	14.1	4.7	20.6	10.5
Denver	5.6	-9.6	7.0	-7.6	9.9	-5.1	15.8	0.2	21.4	5.4
Houston	16.9	7.9	18.4	9.3	21.6	12.0	25.2	16.0	29.1	19.9
Los Angeles	17.7	7.2	17.6	8.2	18.3	9.4	19.4	11.1	20.4	12.9
Miami	24.3	14.4	25.0	14.9	26.6	16.2	28.1	18.8	29.7	20.9
New York	4.3	-2.8	4.1	-2.4	8.9	0.6	14.9	6.1	20.9	10.8
St Louis	4.6	-4.7	6.7	-3.7	11.6	0.2	18.8	6.6	23.9	11.8
Seattle	7.5	2.1	9.4	3.1	11.6	4.2	15.4	6.3	18.8	9.1

Fig. 4. Temperature chart (average maximum and minimum
daily temperatures, ° Celsius).

June		July		Aug.		Sep.		Oct.		Nov.		Dec.	
16.7	9.2	18.4	11.2	17.8	11.1	15.6	9.4	12.1	6.7	8.7	4.1	6.8	2.4
20.3	11.6	21.8	13.5	21.4	13.2	18.5	11.3	14.2	7.9	10.1	5.3	7.3	3.5
16.1	8.3	15.0	7.2	16.7	7.8	18.9	8.9	22.8	10.5	26.1	12.8	28.3	15.0
19.4	5.0	19.4	3.9	22.8	6.1	27.2	9.4	31.1	14.4	33.9	17.7	35.5	20.0
20.5	10.5	20.0	9.4	21.6	10.0	24.4	12.8	26.6	15.5	27.8	17.7	29.4	19.4
11.7	1.1	11.1	0.6	12.8	1.7	16.1	3.3	20.0	6.1	23.9	8.9	26.6	11.7
11.7	11.5	11.1	4.4	12.8	5.0	15.0	6.1	17.2	7.8	18.9	8.9	20.5	10.5
17.7	10.0	17.2	8.9	17.7	8.9	19.4	10.0	21.1	11.7	24.4	13.9	27.2	16.1
16.1	8.9	15.5	7.8	17.2	8.9	19.4	10.5	21.6	13.3	23.3	15.5	25.0	17.2
19.9	8.1	23.6	11.0	21.6	9.2	17.3	4.7	11.1	-0.6	0.0	-8.6	-5.2	-14.2
19.0	9.8	23.2	13.8	23.1	14.4	19.8	11.5	14.2	6.7	8.8	2.1	3.0	-4.1
23.3	14.3	26.1	17.1	24.9	15.9	19.7	11.4	13.5	5.8	5.4	-0.2	-2.5	-8.9
24.2	14.1	27.2	16.8	26.3	16.4	21.6	12.2	14.7	7.2	7.4	1.8	1.1	-4.4
20.0	11.1	22.8	12.8	22.2	12.2	18.9	10.0	13.9	6.7	9.4	3.3	6.7	1.7
14.4	8.9	13.3	7.8	14.4	7.8	15.5	9.4	17.2	11.1	18.9	12.2	21.1	13.9
10.5	2.2	10.0	1.7	11.1	2.2	13.9	4.4	16.7	6.7	18.9	8.3	20.5	10.5
18.0	9.1	17.2	8.4	17.9	9.3	19.3	10.6	21.0	12.4	23.5	14.3	25.2	15.7
15.7	4.0	16.5	4.4	19.3	6.0	22.7	9.0	24.1	11.2	23.9	12.6	24.6	13.6
17.2	7.3	18.6	9.6	17.6	4.2	13.2	4.2	5.7	-2.0	-2.0	-9.2	-6.6	-13.9
26.4	16.4	28.9	19.5	28.0	18.8	23.8	14.1	17.4	8.2	8.4	0.3	2.1	-5.3
27.8	10.6	31.3	14.1	30.4	13.4	26.1	8.3	19.2	2.3	10.9	-4.7	7.3	-7.8
32.4	23.2	33.5	24.2	33.5	24.2	31.2	21.8	27.5	17.3	21.3	11.5	18.1	9.0
22.1	14.7	24.4	16.8	24.1	17.1	24.3	16.2	22.8	13.8	21.7	10.6	19.2	8.5
31.1	23.1	31.6	23.7	32.1	23.8	31.1	23.7	29.3	21.6	26.8	18.1	25.1	15.1
25.6	16.9	28.3	19.9	27.4	19.3	23.8	15.8	18.4	10.3	11.9	4.4	5.7	-1.2
29.5	17.3	31.8	19.4	30.7	19.1	27.4	14.2	21.2	8.1	12.1	1.4	6.1	-3.1
21.3	11.4	24.2	13.2	23.6	13.1	20.7	11.2	15.9	8.4	11.0	4.8	8.8	3.4

Fig. 4. Continued.

WILL YOU GAIN BETTER BUSINESS OR WORK PROSPECTS?

This is a matter that you need to investigate thoroughly. In past decades Britain experienced a brain drain to the United States because the latter had the best research facilities and firms at the leading edge of technology. Yet it is misleading to imagine that the streets of other countries are paved with gold.

A country's fortunes can change radically over the years, and an economy which may have been buoyant a decade ago could be in the doldrums now — and vice versa. New Zealand, once considered a poor relation to Australia, now looks in better economic shape than its larger neighbour.

You need to bear in mind that there can be considerable regional variation, just as there is in the UK. Once prosperous cities, like Detroit in the USA, are currently in decline, while Houston in Texas seems to be riding high — at least for the moment. The last thing you want to do is head for a region where jobs and opportunities are scarce.

Wherever you go you are likely to encounter considerable competition for jobs. To become a successful entrepreneur also requires considerable personal effort. The days when prospects overseas were invariable better are over. Today the European Union (of which the UK is a member) is the largest trading block in the world and as such may well offer opportunities that are as good as anywhere else.

SHOULD YOU AIM FOR EMPLOYMENT OR SELF-EMPLOYMENT?

This seems a good place to consider the pros and cons of setting up in business. If you are starting a new life, why not dispense with the idea of working for a company or organisation and become your own boss?

The countries dealt with in this book welcome entrepreneurs, especially those who have money to invest in businesses which create jobs, and you may well find it easier to qualify for a residence visa as a self-employed business person because less emphasis is placed on formal qualifications. In some cases there may be grants or other concessions available from local or provincial governments which can normally provide you with plenty of useful advice.

However, immigration officials will expect you to have a track record in running a business before they grant the necessary visa. Their caution is understandable: if you have never seen fit to become a businessman in your own country, how can you be expected to launch a successful business in unfamiliar territory?

It can be done, of course, through diligence and hard work. But first you need to research the local market fully to find out if your business idea is really viable. Remember, unless your idea is completely original you will be competing against people who know local trading conditions like the back of their hands. As a newcomer you start out at a disadvantage.

If you are a seasoned business veteran, you will have a much better grasp of what is required in order to get off to a good start. However, you need to be aware that business practices differ from country to country and so do the labour laws. For instance, any hint of discrimination with respect to age, sex or religion in your recruitment of staff could land you in deep water in the United States.

ARE YOU SUITABLE AS AN EMIGRANT?

What can you contribute to the country? This is a question that every potential emigrant is likely to be asked if called for interview and you ought to think very seriously about it. Unsuitable independent migrants may well be weeded out at an early stage by discerning immigration officials.

Those who are sponsored by close relatives will not be subject to such careful scrutiny. Already one country — South Africa — has had second thoughts about family migration since such a large proportion of migrants in this category have failed to secure employment, thus becoming a financial liability to their sponsors. Such problems could arise elsewhere if the economy is in the doldrums.

Let us consider what attributes a model emigrant needs to have.

Good relevant qualifications

The scope for hewers of wood and drawers of water is extremely limited these days; in fact they are not needed at all. The economies of all Western countries have become more sophisticated and now depend increasingly on brainpower rather than musclepower. Manufacturing industry is shedding manpower, while the service sector is expanding. We are fast moving to a post-industrial society in which knowledge is the driving force.

In a society like this, no-one can afford to rest on their laurels. Even if you consider yourself reasonably well qualified, you need to accept that knowledge has a nasty habit of becoming obsolete. As it moves towards the start of the next millennium the country you have selected will have no room for employees who are unskilled, out of date, or whose experience is irrelevant to its needs.

Openmindedness

The country you wish to enter will never be exactly like the one you have left. True, the language may be the same but the accent and some of the expressions will be different; the people may look like you, but there could be subtle differences in their behaviour and attitudes. Australians like to call a spade a spade; Americans can seem pushy and overly patriotic; New Zealanders may seem quaint and old-fashioned. Impressions are all in the eye of the beholder.

If you are sufficiently open-minded you will be able to cope with such differences in temperament and culture.

Tact

Americans feel their country is the greatest in the world, and you will gain no Brownie points in New York if you insist that it isn't. Nor will you be a social success in Sydney if you start comparing Sydney Harbour Bridge unfavourably with the Humber Bridge back home.

Newcomers need to tread very gingerly at first, and you should desist from criticising the government, the facilities or the general way of doing things until you have become established. Even then, you should recognise that the tough guy who is forever slating the government may go on the defensive when a non-native follows suit. A little diplomacy can work wonders in establishing a rapport with nationals of other countries.

Resourcefulness

Would you be able to boil an egg in the Australian outback without the benefit of water? Would you be able to cope if your car got stuck in a six foot snow-drift in the Canadian Rockies? Venture from the main centres of population in some countries and you are left very much to your own devices. DIY skills and the ability to cope in a crisis are useful accomplishments for any would-be emigrant. Besides, in North America particularly, tradesmen such as electricians and plumbers can be hard to find, incompetent, or just very very expensive.

Determination

There may be occasions when you start to harbour doubts as to whether you are doing or have done the right thing, and they could start the moment you file your visa application form. On arrival you may well encounter unexpected difficulties: getting a job may prove harder than you expected, suitable accommodation may be thin on the ground, your family may get homesick, and so might you. The early settlers in the United States and Canada underwent even more traumatic experiences, and it was only their determination to succeed that kept them going. You may need to borrow a few ounces of their determination, too.

Enterprise

Many successful immigrants to Britain are innovative and enterprising people always ready to try something new and prepared to work hard to achieve it. You would do well to emulate their example. Your change of location may well prompt a change in outlook and encourage you to beat the locals at their own game. Instead of looking back to your origins you look forward to future success.

A balanced outlook

Whatever happens you need to keep a sense of perspective. People are not necessarily ganging up on you because they don't respond immediately to your questions. The trouble may stem from the fact that they cannot understand your English accent or they like to size up strangers carefully before getting on first-name terms. There are solutions to every problem and rational explanations for most occurrences, and you should not get upset or jittery in your new surroundings.

Previous experience of the country

Immigration officials often look favourably on people who are, in effect, returnees. If you were born in the country, or once resided there for some time, you may have an automatic right to return. Even if not, if you are familiar with the country, you will be regarded as better able to adapt than a complete newcomer.

A pioneering outlook?

Today when the West has been won and the outback has been tamed there would appear to be very little scope for people to pioneer new settlements and wrestle with nature and the elements. Most emigrants nowadays will make their homes in the suburbs of thriving cities, such as Melbourne, Vancouver or Houston.

Yet there are still areas where a pioneer might feel at home, particularly in Canada. Western Canada and the North West Territory still have vast tracts of wilderness where there are challenges to be met.

WHICH COUNTRY SHOULD YOU OPT FOR?

Having taken a hard look at yourself, your next task is to investigate in the following chapters the country or countries which interest you to see how they measure up to your expectations and requirements.

If you are still unsure as to which country or countries are of greatest interest to you at this stage, the following exercise may help to crystallise your thoughts.

Have a look at chart in Fig. 5 and decide how the country or countries you would like to emigrate to compare with the UK (or your current country of residence) with respect to matters such as climate, education, quality of life, and so on.

If you think the country will be *better* than your own, award one point; if *much better*, award two points. If you think it will be *worse* award minus one; if *much worse*, minus two. Do not award any points if you think it is just the same.

For instance you might award South Africa one point for climate and minus two for law and order; while Canada might score one for education and two for political stability. It may be quite illuminating to add up the totals for the purposes of comparison.

After you have completed the exercise compare notes with someone who knows one or more of the countries really well, and discover how realistic your impressions are.

WHICH REGION OFFERS THE BEST PROSPECTS?

'Nothing you say about the whole country is going to be true,' writes Alistair Cooke about America.[2] The United States covers an enormous land mass which extends through a number of climatic zones. Life on the west coast is different from life on the Atlantic seaboard; and the atmosphere of Chicago is different from that of Miami, New Orleans or Las Vegas.

The same holds true of Canada, Australia — and South Africa, to a certain extent. Alice Springs in Australia does not offer the same amount

	Australia	Canada	New Zealand	South Africa	USA
Climate					
Education					
Quality of life					
Cost of living					
Law and order					
Standard of living					
Economic prospects					
Medical care					
Social differences					
Political stability					
Housing					
Taxation					
TOTAL					

Fig. 5. Chart to test your expectations and requirements.

of sophistication as Sydney; the traditions of Quebec differ markedly from those of Toronto; Durban is altogether a less hectic place than Johannesburg.

So you need to focus your attention not only on the country but on the particular regions in the country which appear to offer the best work prospects, the best facilities, the best climate, the best scenery — or whatever your priorities happen to be.

Notes
[1] J.C. Bossidy, Toast proposed at Harvard dinner, 1910.

[2] *Alistair Cooke's America,* Alistair Cooke (1973).

5
How to Find a Job

It is impossible to enjoy idling thoroughly unless one has plenty of work to do.
(Jerome K. Jerome: *Idle Thoughts of an Idle Fellow*)

Emigrants fall into a number of different categories. Some are going out to join their families — perhaps to assist with the family business or to retire. Others are entering the country as independent immigrants and have no sponsor to sustain them. In the latter case unless you have a substantial income, the need to find gainful employment or a suitable business outlet for your skills will be a top priority.

The strategy you adopt will depend very much on your own personal and financial circumstances. Emigration can turn out to be a costly exercise when immigration fees, travel costs, transport costs and settlement costs are taken into consideration. How much can you invest in finding a worthwhile job as well?

This may seem an unusual question: surely you don't need to pay fees in order to secure employment? Probably not, but you will need to have a financial cushion to support you as you conduct your job search — unless you have a position ready and waiting for you.

If you are planning to start your own business, the financial aspect will be even more important. You will need to get advice — from lawyers, financial and business consultants — and ultimately good advice tends to come with a price tag. You will also require capital — usually substantial amounts of it.

It is never too early to start exploring the job market in the country you wish to move to. Although most countries no longer require immigrants to obtain employment before issuing them with a visa, it is helpful from your point of view if the job-finding process is underway by the time you arrive. Some emigrants like to pay a visit to the country beforehand to find out the lie of the land and make contact with employers and recruitment agencies.

If you put off the job search until you arrive in the country, expect a period of time when you have to live off your own resources. You cannot count on being able to walk into a job on your first day. Just as in the UK, the job-finding process can prove protracted, especially during times of recession and for people in search of more senior jobs.

HOW TO SEARCH FOR A JOB FROM THE UK

There are certain advantages in having a job offer before you leave the UK, or wherever you are currently living. It may, for example, facilitate the granting of a visa; you may get assistance with your travel expenses; and you can start earning a salary immediately you arrive in the country concerned.

You should start by perusing the advertisement columns.

Advertisements in UK newspapers and journals

Although most of the job advertising in these publications are for jobs in the UK you will occasionally find overseas jobs advertised as well. A number of newspapers and professional journals (e.g. *The Times Educational Supplement*) have a special section on overseas jobs. There are also publications which specialise in overseas positions (e.g. *Jobfinder, Nexus, Overseas Jobs Express, Home and Away*) though it has to be admitted that these usually contain few, if any, vacancies in the main countries dealt with in this book.

In many cases the advertisements in UK publications will be for fairly senior posts or in employment sectors suffering from a shortage of skilled personnel (e.g. systems analysts, nurses and paramedics). Some jobs will be on fixed contract terms; others will be open-ended. You can be reasonably confident that the employer is aware of the immigration rules and regulations and has approval to recruit from abroad.

Advertisements in overseas newspapers and journals

Overseas newspapers are more difficult to get hold of, though some embassies, high commissions and provincial/state government offices have reading rooms where you can peruse the newspapers of the country concerned and you may find certain leading journals in large reference libraries (e.g. the City of London Business Library). You could also take out a subscription to the newspaper circulating in the area where you plan to settle. Many overseas newspaper groups have offices in London which can advise you on how to set about this.

While there is no harm in applying for some of the posts you find advertised, you should bear in mind that the advertisements are usually aimed at residents of that particular country not people from overseas, and this places you at a disadvantage. From the employer's point of view a bird in the hand is worth two in a bush, and if a suitable candidate can be found in the immediate locality there is little point in considering applications form far afield.

If your qualifications are exceptional and the post a particularly high-powered one it could a different matter. Furthermore, if you are planning a visit to the country in the near future and offer to pay the firm a visit, the selectors might take a greater interest in you.

I am not suggesting that you ignore overseas newspapers entirely. A glance though the classified columns of these newspapers will give you an idea of which skills are in demand and what salaries are being offered — information which will help you come to a realistic decision.

Speculative job searching

Advertisements are just one of the methods employed by firms and organisations to recruit staff. Not all firms do it. If they know of suitable people who can fill their vacancies there is little need for them to advertise. What *you* have to do is ensure they know about *you*, and this means seizing the initiative.

Most of the techniques outlined below depend on desk research in reference libraries and the like. There are reference books, such as the *Kompass* series, which list the firms of particular countries by activity and geographical location.

If you find such reference works formidable, see if you can track down the relevant foreign telephone directory. If you are a mechanical engineer keen to emigrate to Manitoba, your first step might be to look in the Manitoba *Yellow Pages* for firms and employment agencies that could be of help.

Networking

This means making use of your contacts. Have you any relations, friends or business contacts overseas who may be able to suggest jobs you should try for or even be in a position to offer you employment? If so, a friendly letter or telephone call is in order, followed up by a detailed CV.

You need not confine yourself to people you know. If you belong to a trade union or professional association, why not inform its secretary of your plans and ask him or her to provide you with contacts overseas?

Twinning links should also be exploited: some towns and cities in the UK have strong ties with places in other countries, particularly those with similar names. Liverpuddlians, for instance, might write off to the Chamber of Commerce in Liverpool, New South Wales, or Mancunians to the mayor of Manchester, New Hampshire, to find out about job prospects in those parts of the world. Ask your local council for a few contacts.

Recruitment consultants

Recruitment consultants act as intermediaries for companies and organisations. They often place advertisements for their clients and may do the initial selection for the shortlist. A number of consultancies in this country welcome speculative applications, and if they have no suitable positions at the time they will often be happy to place your particulars on file.

The majority of recruitment consultants (employment agencies, executive search agencies) do not recruit for positions overseas, even if they are part of an international chain. They may, however, be able to supply you with the names and addresses of sister companies in the country you are interested in.

On the other hand there are some agencies that do handle overseas positions or particular countries. They may specialise in certain disciplines (e.g. medical, computer personnel) or on particular countries, and so you should select your consultant with care. A specialist in the recruitment of construction personnel for the Middle East is unlikely to be of any assistance to an accountant wishing to emigrate to Australia.

Members of the Federation of Recruitment and Employment Services are listed in the overseas section of the Federation's Yearbook. Handbooks such as *How to Get a Job Abroad, How to Get a Job in America* and *How to Get a Job in Australia* also list such firms.

The Executive Grapevine, the CEPEC Recruitment Guide and *International Directory of Executive Recruitment Consultants* list organisations which handle fairly senior positions, though not all of these recruit for overseas positions. A number of these specialise in executive search, sometimes known as 'headhunting', and if you are seeking a job in the £60,000 plus bracket you should make sure they have your particulars.

It is worth noting that under UK law recruitment consultants operating in this country are not allowed to charge fees to job applicants; their fee income is derived from the employers that engage them to recruit staff. If you come across one that attempts to charge you, you should tread very warily and inform the Department of Trade and Industry which licenses these consultancies. You should also be wary of premium rate phone lines which promise overseas job information and cost you dearly.

Jobsearch and immigration consultants

There are a number of organisations, such as Jobsearch and LEADS, which assist would-be immigrants with finding a job, and it would be worthwhile approaching some of them to see if they can offer the kind of service that you want. They advertise in migrant newspapers and the appointment sections of the national press.

Some like Walker and Walker offer lists of employers and employment agencies in the countries of locations where you wish to settle; others offer advice and can put you in contact with people in the recruitment business overseas. In some cases interviews can be arranged with prospective employers.

In Chapter 3 mention is made of immigration consultants who assist in submitting visa applications. A number of these also offer assistance in securing employment as well through their network of contacts. The Directory at the end of this book lists a number of addresses.

UK-based companies

Many international companies with a substantial UK base recruit globally for many of their senior staff. If you work for such a company and have specialist skills, opportunities may arise for you to be transferred overseas. However, there is no guarantee that this will happen or that you will be able to choose where you are sent to.

Speculative applications to such companies asking to be considered for vacancies in such-and-such a country are unlikely to bear fruit. You may fare better if you concentrate on companies whose principal activities are overseas — companies in the oil and mining sectors are a good example. Previous experience of living and working in a particular country may also help you achieve your goal.

As door-to-door salesmen will doubtless confirm, cold calling can be a depressing activity. You have to knock on so many doors in order to achieve one positive response. You can shorten the odds somewhat by doing extensive research and targeting only those employers that look promising.

Companies overseas

Imagine you are the human resource manager (personnel officer) of Levy Sablosky Sato Inc. (a fictitious company, I hope) of Bakersfield, California and you receive a speculative application from a person living five or six thousand miles away. You have no vacancies, and even if you had, would you even consider recruiting from Europe when you have a multi-talented workforce on your doorstep? It is hardly worth even replying to the aspirant.

Cold calling from a great distance seldom bears fruit. Even a person from the Atlantic seaboard of the United States who is free to work anywhere in the United States would probably receive similar treatment from a Bakersfield firm, unless a very senior position has to be filled.

Imagine, however, that the writer of the letter mentions that he is visiting California the following month and would like to drop into discuss the possibility of a job. Since no-one at Levy Sablosky Sato has ever set eyes on a person from the British Isles before, your curiosity is aroused and you invite him or her to call by, though you can't promise anything.

A personal appearance can often be more effective than a written application, no matter how well it is crafted. This is a theme that I shall now treat at greater length.

JOB SEARCH VISITS

Attempting to find a job from a great distance is fraught with problems, and even if you are successful, you can never be sure that you have made the right choice until you actually arrive. (Some candidates may be invited overseas for the final interview, but this normally happens only for senior posts.)

Conducting your job search within the country of settlement is infinitely preferable, and my guess is that the majority of migrants put off finding a job until after their arrival. This is fine if you have relations and friends who can put you up as a temporary measure, your outgoings are fairly low and you manage to find a job quickly.

Unfortunately, things do not always work out as you might wish. You cannot always count on finding a position immediately; it can take weeks, even months, especially if you are after a fairly senior post. If the economy is in recession and you have settled in an unemployment black-spot, securing employment can take even longer.

It is no use hanging about hoping that the right position at the right level will materialise. Indeed if your funds are running low you may well have to compromise and accept a less senior post than you hoped for, purely to get a foot on the employment ladder. Remember that once you leave the UK you are normally no longer eligible for supplementary benefits, and not all countries have a system of unemployment benefit for newcomers.

If you have not been successful in landing a job from the UK, it would be worth your while to make a short visit to the country concerned before you move and see as many prospective employers, recruitment consultancies and other contacts as you can. Bear in mind, however, that while you might be able to cover much of New Zealand in a fortnight, you will only be able to take in a part of Canada or the United States — unless you have your own private jet.

To derive the maximum advantage of such a trip, forward planning is vital. You will need to do your homework before you go, deciding which organisations and firms are worth trying and setting up appointments in advance. This means plenty of persuasive letters accompanied by impressive CVs — followed up by telephone calls. Some migration and job search consultancies may be able to set up appointments for you or suggest contacts; international recruitment agencies may be happy to put you in touch with their affiliates.

Many local authorities have business reference libraries which have foreign telephone directories and business directories (e.g. Kompass). Londoners might try the City Business Library in Brewers' Hall Garden, the City of Westminster Reference Library just off Leicester Square, or the libraries of the appropriate diplomatic missions. (Not all of the latter offer access to the general public and it is advisable to contact them in advance.)

BUSINESS VISITS

If you are planning to start or invest in a business you will probably need to pay more than one visit before you decide to take the plunge. You will need to get to know the precise lie of the land and discuss your project with as many people as possible. In some cases you may be able to get help from government offices in the form of grants and tax concessions, but you usually need to stake your claim before you act.

Whether you are investing in a firm, buying a business or starting from scratch you need to be fully acquainted with business practice and employment legislation. While there are similarities with the way businesses are run in Britain, there are differences as well, and if you do not take note of these you could be heading for legal problems or potential bankruptcy.

You therefore need to avail yourself of all the help that is available. Call on the nearest British Embassy, High Commission or Consulate (if you are a UK citizen) and talk to the trade attaché. He (or she) will be able to advise you on business prospects in the country or region and suggest useful contacts — chambers of commerce, lawyers, business advisers, and so on.

In some larger centres there will be a British Chamber of Commerce run by expatriate business people who know the ropes and are usually glad to lend a compatriot a helping hand. The economic development boards

(or similarly named organisations) of state, provincial and city governments are often extremely keen to offer advice to people who are prepared
to invest in certain kinds of business.

However, the final decision is yours, and you should not embark on
any business venture unless you are really certain that you can bring it off.

DELAYING THE JOB SEARCH

Some emigrants prefer to put off the job search until they actually arrive
in a country. If you have skills which you know are in great demand in
the place you are bound for (e.g. computer or accountancy skills) there
could be advantages in doing this. You will then be able to apply to a
number of firms and choose from a number of offers. (This process is dealt
with at greater length in Chapter 7.)

However, most people would be best advised against putting off the
evil day when you have to get down to looking for work. Mention has
already been made of the fact that the selection process can take months,
during which time your savings can become severely depleted. Even if
you have not managed to secure a job you should have established some
leads beforehand which you can follow up soon after your arrival.

Case study
When HN and her fiancé arrived in Western Australia they assumed they
would pick up jobs quite easily since they both had useful skills. However
unemployment was high and jobs — even temporary ones — were few
and far between. Moreover, she felt at a disadvantage since she was a
newcomer. After three months without work she received a job offer from
Queensland, and they had to decide whether to spend the rest of their
savings on moving to Queensland or returning home. In the event they
returned to the UK where they both picked up jobs easily. 'It might have
been better if we had arranged jobs before we left Britain,' she reflects.

6
Preparing for the Move

Nearly a quarter of a million people leave the United Kingdom every year to work abroad for periods ranging from a few months to the remainder of their normal working lives. The vast majority of them go away having made less preparation for what faces them than when they last spent a fortnight in Benidorm or Tenerife. (Harry Brown and Rosemary Thomas, *Brits Abroad*)[1]

If you are leaving Britain for good, you will need to start preparing for the move weeks or even months in advance. This chapter lists the most important points, but does not claim to be definitive. Personal circumstances will dictate which matters are of relevance to you, and it would be sensible first to skim through the items in this chapter and mark those which you feel deserve your attention.

ARRANGING YOUR ARRIVAL

When you arrive at a strange airport after a long flight it is always a great relief to find someone there to meet you and help you get settled in. However, this will only happen if you inform your contacts of your flight details (i.e. flight number and estimated time of arrival). You should also make sure that you have their full address and a phone number to ring in case of unexpected hitches.

If you have no relative, friend or employer to pick you up at the other end other arrangements are possible. If you are already using the services of a migration consultancy they may be able to arrange for you to be met on arrival and put into temporary accommodation, if necessary. Alternatively, you could ask your travel agent or airline to book you into a hotel for a few nights: some hotels offer a transport service from the airport for their clients.

In some countries there are companies which offer a 'meet and greet service' (their advertisements appear in immigrant newspapers), while organisations such as Christians Abroad and the Church of England Board for Social Responsibility (Overseas Settlement Secretary) can arrange for members of local churches to help you settle in.

BANKING

Don't take a suitcase of banknotes abroad with you. Thanks to improvements in banking technology anyone who has a credit card, charge card or cash/payment card (such as Delta or Switch) can obtain cash from banks or buy goods in many countries of the world. It is worth while keeping your UK credit card account open, as it can take time to open a similar account with a bank elsewhere.

Travellers' cheques are always useful — for the USA they should always be denominated in US dollars — and it would be sensible to obtain a small amount of foreign currency as well for small payments on arrival; the last thing you will want to do at your port of entry is queue up at a bureau de change. You should also investigate the possibility of transferring cash to a back at your destination.

When you get to your destination the likelihood is that you will need to open a bank account there for which you will need a reference from your current bank. Alternatively, you may find it possible to open an account with an overseas bank before you leave the UK. However, make sure that the bank you choose operates on a nationwide basis. American banks, for instance, do not.

Several Commonwealth and South African banks have branches in London with specialised departments that deal with migrants. A number, such as the Commonwealth Bank of Australia, produce useful brochures with details of house prices and the cost of living, and may also offer briefings on financial matters to migrants before they leave.

What about your UK bank account? It makes sense to keep it going — at least, for the time being — even if you decide to transfer most of your financial assets abroad. It can be useful if you return to the UK on holiday or if you need to make payments in sterling. You need, however, to ensure that the account is kept topped up, and should keep your bank informed of your movements and your contact address(es); and in the case of South Africa you should take care not to contravene exchange control regulations.

BRIEFINGS

No matter how well you have prepared for your move there may be questions for which you and your dependants seek answers. For instance:

- What kind of electrical appliances should I take with me and will they work on the local current?

- Can you buy mustard and Branston pickle in local supermarkets?

- What is the best way to get into town from the airport?

- How competent are local garages and would they know how to service my 1950 Bentley?

- Are there any competent tailors in X, or is it better for me to buy all my clothes before I go?

- What do I wear if the boss invites me to a cocktail party?

- Do local newsagents sell *Country Life, Beano* and other British publications?

- Which bank offers the best service and has the lowest charges?

In Chapter 4 various sources of information are recommended, including location reports, briefing notes and books on life in various countries. Unfortunately you are unlikely to find answers to every question in these, and you may welcome an opportunity to talk to someone with recent experience of the country you are moving to. Clearly if you have relations or friends overseas they can give you the advice you need, or perhaps you know someone in the UK who can fill you in. If you are making use of the services of a migration counsellor a briefing may form part of the service. Another idea is to use the services of a briefing agency. They include:

- Women's Corona Society/Corona International: offers face-to-face or telephone briefings in addition to their seminar programme

- Employment Conditions Abroad: offers face-to-face briefings for individuals or couples in addition to their normal seminar programme

- Centre for International Briefing: runs regular seminars on different countries tailored to the needs of participants.

CANCELLATIONS AND DISCONNECTIONS

You will need to cancel

● milk delivery
● newspaper delivery
● subscriptions to magazines or clubs you are no longer interested in
● rental agreements (e.g. TV).

You will also need to notify the companies providing the following services of your date of departure and arrange for the payment of bills:

● electricity
● gas
● telephone
● water.

If you are renting accommodation you need to inform your landlord that you wish to terminate the lease.

CAR

If you are a driver, you will doubtless wish to have your own private transport in your overseas location. There are various options open to you.

Take your present car out with you

You need to consider the age of the car: if it is several years old, it will cost more to maintain, and obtaining spare parts could be a problem. You will also need to make sure that it complies with regulations in the country where you plan to reside, since modification could prove expensive. Shipping it out could also prove costly, and you should check what taxes or import duties will be payable at the other end. It is worth noting that sending a vehicle by container may prove more costly than by the roll-on-roll-off method.

The Department of Transport leaflet V526 gives details of how to export a car you already own. If you are taking it out for more than a year, when you actually leave you should complete Section 2 on the back of the Vehicle Registration Document and send it to the Driver Vehicle and Licensing Centre in Swansea. You may be lucky enough to get a refund of excess duty paid.

Buy a new car in the UK

If you are keen to have a model that is not available in the country of settlement, you might well decide to purchase a new car. Otherwise — and this applies particularly to Canada, Australia and the United States which have their own automobile industries — there is not much point.

It is possible to buy a car in the UK free of VAT provided you export it within six months; and your car dealer can provide you with the necessary VAT Form 410. You should specify where you intend to use the car, and the agent will ensure that you get a model which complies with the legal requirements of the country in question.

You should investigate what the freight charges, customs duties and other taxes will amount to, and also how easy it is to obtain spare parts.

Buy a new car in the country where you intend to live

This may prove to be the most sensible option, particularly if you are heading for Australia, Canada or the United States. All these countries have indigenous car manufacturers whose products are very competitively priced. South Africa manufactures cars too, but they are currently subject to very high VAT rates.

CHILDREN

If your children are of school age you need to make arrangements for their schooling. If you are planning to enrol them in a state school you should write to the Department of Education — in the appropriate state, where the country is federal — requesting a list of schools and further information. Alternatively, the cultural attaché at the relevant diplomatic mission may be able to advise you.

Most countries also have an extensive private sector, and if you feel that your children would benefit from being educated at a private school, you should make enquiries. Some diplomatic missions will have directories of private schools which you can consult; otherwise you could write to the national governing body or association for private schools or (in the case of denominational schools) the religious organisation to which you belong. Word of mouth is usually the best kind of recommendation, so if you have contacts overseas you should ask them which schools have a good reputation.

Some of the best private schools have long waiting lists (like Eton) and you should therefore not put off enrolment until the last moment, or your offspring may fail to gain a place in the school of your choice. Most schools will expect children to start attending at the beginning of the school year, and in this regard you should note that in the southern hemisphere the school year starts in February.

Complications can arise if your children have reached a crucial stage in their education where important examinations are imminent. You might consider deferring your move, but this is not always feasible, in which case it is essential to discuss the options with your offspring, their current teachers and perhaps your local education authority (if they are attending state schools), in order to minimise disruption to their education. Educational consultancies, such as Dean Associates, can also advise.

Generally, speaking all the countries dealt with in this book have excellent schools, but not all are of a high standard. If you are keen for your children to stay in the UK for their education a way can usually be found. You could, for instance, appoint a guardian — a relation, friend or organisation offering guardianship services (such as GJW and Gabbitas Truman & Thring) — to look after their interests in the UK.

There are a number of organisations which can offer you advice on private schools in the UK, notably Gabbitas Truman & Thring and the Independent Schools Information Service (ISIS). You could also consult *The Parents' Guide to Independent Schools*, published by the School Fees Insurance Agency (SFIA). If you require independent advice on higher and further education opportunities in the UK, the privately owned Higher Education and Planning Service can offer up-to-date information.

Should you be planning to settle in a remote area where you suspect the quality of the schooling is poor, you could have a crack at educating your children yourself. Worldwide Education Services (WES) can provide you with training, materials and support for children up to 13 years old and no prior experience of teaching is required. For older children you could investigate correspondence tuition from an organisation like Mercer's College which specialises in correspondence courses up to 'A' Level, though this form of learning is no easy option. However, you may well find that there are distance learning facilities closer at hand.

CLOTHING

There is little point in investing in a completely new wardrobe before you leave unless items are of poor quality, expensive or unavailable at your destination. Of greater importance is to pack the right kind of clothing to take with you. If you are heading for the southern hemisphere (Australia, South Africa and New Zealand), bear in mind that the seasons are the opposite to those in northern Europe, and take some warm clothes with you if you leave in the summer and summer clothes if you are departing in the winter. For a lengthy flight, dress comfortably (but not scruffily) rather than elegantly.

DRIVING LICENCE

You should take your driving licence with you as you will need to show it when you apply for a licence at your destination. You might also consider obtaining a one-year international driving licence from the AA or RAC, particularly if you are planning to drive in other countries.

ELECTORAL REGISTRATION

If you wish to vote in elections held in the UK while you are abroad, you need to ask the electoral registration officer of your local district or borough council for a change of address form. This entitles you to appoint a proxy to vote for you in any parliamentary, European and local election for the duration of the current electoral register. In order keep your voting rights in future years you need to contact the nearest British Embassy or Consulate after your arrival and complete the necessary form.

You should note that you will not normally be entitled to vote in major elections at your destination unless you become naturalised.

FINANCIAL ADVICE

Moving overseas permanently will have important implications for your finances, and the more assets you have the more complicated your situation is likely to be.

For example, you may wish to dispose of your home in the UK in order to purchase accommodation overseas. While your main home is exempt from capital gains tax if you sell while you are still a UK resident in the eyes of the Inland Revenue, what happens if it is not sold before you take up residence abroad? Will you be subject to capital gains tax in your new country of residence? Or if you have been paying into a pension fund you may want to find out whether it is transferable and whether there are any tax concessions in your country of destination.

Taxation needs to be gone into, not only UK taxation but the tax regime in your prospective country of residence. For while you may be perfectly conversant with the UK tax system, the rules and regulations in other countries could differ quite markedly. To understand the implications more clearly consult books such as *The Allied Dunbar Expatriate Tax Guide* or Ernst and Young's *Worldwide Personal Tax Guide*.

Alternatively or additionally, you should seek out a qualified adviser on expatriate finance at the earliest possible opportunity. Your bank may have a department dealing with expatriates, you could ask the local branch of the Society of Chartered Accountants to recommend an international taxation expert in your area or you could approach one of the firms listed in the directory at the end of this book.

It is often better to use an adviser who charges for his or her advice than someone who gives free advice in anticipation of being able to sell you a financial product on which he or she earns a commission. Note also that when it comes to buying financial products in the UK there are two categories of advisers:

● independent advisers who recommend the best product on the market, no matter which company provides it

● 'tied' advisers who recommend only the products of the company that they represent.

See also entries in this chapter on Insurance, Investment, Pension, Taxation.

FORWARDING OF MAIL

No matter how hard you try to let everybody know of your change of address you may well find that some mail continues to arrive at your old home. You may be able to make an arrangement with the new owners or tenants to forward your mail, but it may be more satisfactory to ask the post office to undertake this chore for a limited period. This involves completing a form obtainable from any post office and paying a small fee.

If you do not have a forwarding address, letters can be sent poste restante c/o the post office in the town or city where you will be living, or you could enquire about having a PO box.

YOUR HOME IN THE UK

Most emigrants who own their own homes decide to sell up in order to finance the purchase of a new property at their destination. In recent years the property market has been depressed and some people have had to delay their move until they have managed to sell their property.

You must bear in mind that once you have received the necessary permission to emigrate you cannot delay your departure indefinitely since your visa will normally have an expiry date. So it is advisable to put the house up for sale as soon as the approval of your application to emigrate comes through.

You can advertise it yourself or enlist the help of an estate agent. There are several excellent books on buying and selling houses and flats in the UK, such as *Which Way to Buy, Sell and Move House* from the Consumers' Association, so the topic will not be dealt with here.

If you have difficulty in disposing of it, you could consider letting it for a period until such time that it is sold. If you have engaged an estate agent to handle the sale he or she may be able to arrange the letting for you, though there will be a fee, and your letting income will be taxable by the Inland Revenue.

What a letting agent can do
- advertise for tenants
- interview prospective tenants
- take up references
- draw up leasing agreement and serve relevant notices
- draw up inventories
- visit properties and attend to any complaints or queries
- collect rent
- serve notice to quit and attend court
- attend to building repairs and any major building work
- account to clients by way of statements and payment of rents
- pay water rates and other charges
- negotiate rent increases
- deal with insurance claims
- deal with the Inland Revenue if your letting income attracts tax.

INSURANCE

You need to consider both your short-term and long-term insurance needs, especially if you have a family.

Travel insurance
This is essential not only for yourself but also your personal effects. You may arrive safely, but your luggage whether accompanied or unaccompanied could arrive damaged, or worse still, not arrive at all. The removal firm which handles the transport of your bulkier items may provide insurance as part of the removal package. (See Removals.)

Medical insurance

Few countries have a comprehensive state health-care system on the lines of the National Health, and you need to find out precisely what benefits (if any) are offered and whether they would apply to you. If you have any doubts it would be sensible to take out a temporary medical insurance policy (which might form part of your travel insurance) to see you through your first month or perhaps longer. On arrival at your destination it would be wise to investigate local practice.

Life assurance

If you have dependants, it is possible that you already have a life assurance policy which would provide cash for your family in the event of your decease. You now need to review your policy in the light of your changing circumstances. Is it, for instance, sensible to continue with this particular policy or are there advantages to be gained in changing?

Other insurance

If you plan to drive overseas you will have to obtain insurance cover at your destination, which will doubtless work out more expensive than in the UK. To keep down costs, you should ask your current insurance company for a letter confirming your no-claims-bonus record. It might be wise to do the same for your house and contents insurance.

INVESTMENTS

This is a good time to review your investments, though just because you are moving, there is no need to transfer all your capital overseas unless you are really going to need it. Indeed, in the case of South Africa with its strict exchange controls you may well decide to transfer only a portion of your assets. Some investors find it advantageous to put some of their cash into well-regulated off-shore tax havens (e.g. the Channel Isles or the Isle of Man) and you could investigate whether such a move would be advantageous to you.

Two points worth bearing in mind are:

● Don't change your investments simply for the sake of change, particularly if they are performing well.

● Make sure that your investments are in more than one currency. In the past people living overseas with cash in sterling deposit accounts have suffered as a result of the pound's devaluation.

LEGAL MATTERS

If you are selling property or a business, the chances are that you will be meeting your solicitor anyway before you go, so that you can give him or her a forwarding address. This might be a good time to make a will, to appoint someone with power of attorney and deal with any other legal matters that might crop up.

The chances are that your UK lawyer will not be in a position to advise you on property transactions at your destination, but he or she may be able to put you in touch with a reputable practitioner there.

MEDICAL MATTERS

You need to investigate whether to take any precautionary measures before you leave Britain, and it is sensible to visit those who have looked after your health in recent years. You will find plenty of useful advice on going abroad in the Department of Health booklet *Health Advice for Travellers* obtainable free of charge from chemists, doctors, DSS offices or by phoning 0800 555777. The information is also available on Prestel Page 50063.

The following suggestions will ensure that you get off to a good start.

Have appropriate vaccinations

At present no special vaccinations are needed for North America or Australasia, but precautions against polio, typhoid, hepatitis A and malaria are recommended for South Africa and your course of treatment may need to start as much as two months before your departure. Such precautions may also be needed if you plan to stop off en route.

The booklet *Health Advice for Travellers* should tell you what you need to know. For a more comprehensive health brief (for which a fee is payable) you should contact Medical Advisory Services for Travellers Abroad (MASTA). MASTA application forms are also obtainable from some chemists.

Your doctor or local health centre may be able to vaccinate you, but you may find it more convenient to use one of the British Airways Travel Clinics in Birmingham, Edinburgh, Glasgow, Leicester, Manchester, Newport Pagnell, Nottingham, Purley, Reading, Stratford on Avon and London. These are linked to the MASTA database. Telephone (071) 831 5333 for further details.

Visit your doctor

It is sensible to visit your GP to tell him or her of your plans and ideally have a check up. The immigration authorities may require you to be medically examined before granting you an entry visa, and your GP may be able to carry this out. Normally a fee is payable for this service even if you are an NHS patient.

If you are on medication make sure that you are given a letter to show customs officers on arrival, since some countries place restrictions on the import of certain drugs. You also need to discuss arrangements for the transfer of your medical records.

Visit your dentist

This is a good time to have a dental check-up or arrange to have spare dentures made. Dental treatment can be quite expensive abroad and it is not usually covered by national health schemes.

Visit the optician

It is also a good idea to have your eyes tested, and if you are going to a sunny clime you may want to have a pair of tinted spectacles.

Buy medical supplies

It is always sensible to take your own health kit with you for use on the journey or on arrival, more especially if you are travelling with children. I would suggest:

● cotton wool
● antiseptic cream
● aspirin (or other painkiller)
● Elastoplast
● insect repellent
● travel sickness pills
● diarrhoea pills
● indigestion tablets
● sun cream.

Some firms and organisations market first-aid kits (e.g. Elastoplast and the British Red Cross), though none of them contains all these recommendations. It would also be sensible to take with you a first-aid booklet ot, better still, a medical book on the lines of *Travellers' Health*, Richard Dawood (OUP).

Surrender your NHS card

Your can either send this to the local Family Practitioner Committee or hand it to the passport official as you leave the country. It is advisable to keep a note of the number in case you return to the UK on a long-term basis.

Once you have emigrated you may discover that you are not entitled to NHS treatment on return visits to the UK, and will need to take out private medical insurance for such occasions. However, if you return for good you will normally become eligible once more. You should consult the relevant Benefits Agency leaflet. (See National Insurance.)

NATIONAL INSURANCE

You should contact the DSS Benefits Agency (Overseas Branch) in Newcastle for advice on National Insurance contributions stating where you plan to emigrate to. It may be to your advantage to pay voluntary contributions at the Class 3 (non-employed) rate to maintain your UK insurance record for the retirement pension and widow's benefits, especially if you plan ultimately to return to the UK.

These voluntary payments, however, will not necessarily entitle you to social security benefits in your new country of residence, and you will probably need either to contribute to the state insurance scheme there or to take out private insurance. Since individual circumstances differ, it is impossible to offer general advice in this book, and you should therefore clarify your position with both the Overseas Branch and the social security organisation at your destination in order to reach an informed decision.

Britain has a social security agreement with a number of different countries but the terms of the agreements vary. Make sure you obtain a copy of the relevant leaflet from the DSS Overseas Branch in Newcastle upon Tyne (Australia: SA5; Canada: SA20; New Zealand SA8; USA: SA33). There is no agreement with South Africa.

PASSPORT AND VISA

If your British passport is due to expire fairly soon you ought to renew it before you submit it to the visa department of the relevant embassy or high commission. You can obtain a form from your local post office or else visit the passport office in person. Here are the addresses of the Passport Office:

Personal callers only
Clive House, 70 Petty France, London SW1H 9HD. Tel: (071) 279 3434.

Postal and personal applications
5th Floor, India Buildings, Water Street, Liverpool L2 0QZ. Tel: (051) 237 3010 (North of England and North Wales).
Olympia House, Upper Dock Street, Newport, Gwent NP9 1XA. Tel: (0633) 244500/244292 (South Wales, South and West).
Aragon Court, Northminster Road, Peterborough PE1 1QG. Tel: (0733) 895555 (Midlands, East Anglia and Kent).
3 Northgate, 96 Milton Street, Cowcaddens, Glasgow G4 0BT. Tel: (041) 332 0271 (Scotland, London and Middlesex).
Hampton House, 47–53 High Street, Belfast BT1 2QS. Tel: (0232) 232371 (Northern Ireland).

Once you have your passport, you can send it with your application to the appropriate embassy or high commission. The procedures are dealt with in the appropriate chapters for each country in this book. Even if you employ an agent to make the arrangements for you, you may be required to attend the embassy or high commission in person at some stage.

As well as your passport you may well have to produce some, or all, of the following items:

- birth certificate
- marriage certificate
- evidence of financial status
- sworn affidavit attesting that you have no criminal convictions
- medical report
- photographs
- references
- certificates showing your qualifications. (If copies are sent they may have to be authenticated by a solicitor or notary.)

PENSION

You have the right to continue making voluntary NI payments (Class 2 or 3) which will count towards your UK pension. It can be beneficial to do so if you feel that you may return to the UK at some time in the future. However, it may be a less attractive option if you expect to retire eventually to a country where this pension is frozen (notably, Australia, Canada, New Zealand and South Africa). Bear in mind that you may well have to contribute to a state or private pension scheme in your country of settlement.

If you are already a pensioner, you should inform the Benefits Agency (Overseas Branch) of the Department of Social Security of your new address and anticipated date of departure, and arrange how your state pension is to be paid — normally either by credit transfer or a monthly sterling cheque.

Unfortunately, if you are heading for Australia, Canada, New Zealand and South Africa, your pension will be frozen (i.e. it will not be uprated annually in the line with inflation), so various pressure groups are currently lobbying for a change in the new law. The administrators of any private or occupational pension fund of which you are a member should also be informed of your movements. (See *How to Retire Abroad*.)

You may well have been contributing to an occupational pension scheme in the UK, in which case you need to investigate what happens when you move overseas. While your pension may be transferable, the chances are that it is not, in which case you may need to seek advice from a pensions adviser with international experience.

If you subscribe to a personal pension fund you need to investigate the implications of moving abroad. You may, for instance, no longer receive tax concessions on your premiums and there may be restrictions on investing in a UK pension fund. On the brighter side there could be advantages in moving it offshore. You should also check whether you will be required to make contributions to an occupational pension fund when you take up work overseas.

PETS

If you decide to take your pet with you, you need to comply with the rules and regulations of the country you are going to, and its embassy or high commission can give you details. This normally entails obtaining a certificate from the local veterinary inspector of the Ministry of Agriculture, Fisheries and Food (the address will be in the local telephone directory) stating

- the species and breed of the animal
- that it has been examined and found free from all signs and symptoms of infectious and contagious diseases.

Dogs need to be vaccinated against rabies not less than 15 days before you leave, and your vet will need to get authorisation to obtain the vaccine from the Ministry's Divisional Veterinary Officer. Further information is available from MAFF, Animal Health Division IC in Surrey.

There are a number of organisations which specialise in transporting pets abroad, and some addresses will be found in the directory at the end of this book. It may be possible for your pet to travel on the same flight as you, though not in the passenger compartment. However some countries insist that they are sent unaccompanied. In either case the pet will need a specially designed container. The RSPCA and British Airways World Cargo publish leaflets on taking pets abroad.

Not all pets are keen to move and, besides, they may well have to undergo a period in quarantine on their arrival overseas. Especially if your animals are getting long in the tooth, it may be kinder to leave them in the UK provided you can find a good home for them. There are several animal charities that may be able to assist in this (e.g. Cats Protection Society, National Canine Defence League, and so on). Your local telephone directory will list your nearest branch.

If you return to the UK and bring your pets with you, it is highly likely that they will have to go into quarantine for six months.

POWER OF ATTORNEY

If you have unfinished business (e.g. a property to sell, a business to wind up) it may be sensible to appoint someone who can act on your behalf (e.g. sign documents, pay bills and so on). Normally this involves the drawing up of a legal agreement.

REMOVALS

Will it be cheaper to ship all your household effects to your destination or should you sell everything and buy new when you arrive? This is one of the burning issues you will need to address. You may well settle on a compromise: you ship out items which are valuable or not easily replaceable, and purchase the balance at your destination.

Moving one's personal effects from one country to another is a complicate business and often involves a number of different contractors. You will be paying for a number of services.

Packing

Items need to be packed properly otherwise they could be broken in transit. The insurance company may not pay out on claims if the packing has not been done professionally.

Preparation of documents

There will be forms to be filled in and an inventory to be made to satisfy customs.

- collection and delivery to port
- transport by sea (rarely by air unless the items are small)
- customs clearance
- storage
- collection from port and delivery to your new home
- insurance.

While it is possible to undertake some of these tasks yourself, the best plan is to entrust the whole matter to an international removal firm which can undertake door to door delivery. Such a firm needs to be bonded with the British Association of Removers Overseas or the Association of International Removers. Membership of OMNI (the Overseas Moving Network Inc.) or FIDI (the International Federation of International Furniture Removers) is a further indication of competence. It is advisable to contact more than one firm to obtain some competitive quotes.

The moving scenario will normally unfold in the following way:

- The firm sends an assessor to your home to estimate the volume of items to be transported.

- A few days later you will receive a quotation in which charges for different services are itemised together with an inventory (which must be checked carefully for omissions).

- The items have to be valued for insurance and customs purposes. Insurance values must be based on the replacement value.

- A date is arranged for the items to be packed and collected.

Reputation and price will be important considerations in choosing a removal firm. You should also ask the following questions:

- Does the company do its own professional packing or employ sub-contractors?

- Does the company make its own direct shipping arrangements without the involvement of third-party forwarders/agents?

● Does the company have branches in the country you are emigrating to? If not, who is the agent?

● Can the company explain customs and quarantine requirements and give details of restricted articles?

In most cases the items will be shipped in containers and the quotation will be based on a container load. If you do not have sufficient personal effects to fill a container, part loads are possible, or tea chests could be used.

TAXATION

When you emigrate you are changing from one tax regime to another. Before you leave the UK you need to contact the Inland Revenue to inform them of your move. If you convince the tax inspectors you are going away for good, you should get a rebate on overpaid income tax. However you will need to inform them of your contact address, as this may not happen immediately.

When you are living outside the UK you may find that you are still liable for UK tax on various forms of income arising within the country, including most investment income and income from property (e.g. rent). You could also be taxed on capital gains, and should therefore take advice on how to minimise your liability.

However, before you even approach a taxation expert you would be wise to contact the Inland Revenue Claims Branch (Foreign Division) in Bootle who produce a number of useful booklets, viz.

● IR6 Double Taxation Relief
● IR58 Going to work abroad
● IR20 Residents and Non-Residents.

If you are all at sea after reading these, you can contact the Foreign Division again and they will answer your queries (in writing or over the phone) or refer to the Inspector of Foreign Dividends in Nottingham, if appropriate.

You should also find out about your tax liabilities in the country in which you will be living. The high commission or embassy should be able to provide you with details, or you could refer to Ernst and Young's *Worldwide Personal Tax Guide*

Is there a risk of paying tax twice over? Fortunately, no. Britain has signed double taxation agreements with Australia, Canada, New Zealand, South Africa and the USA. (See leaflet IR6.)

TRAVEL ARRANGEMENTS

The days when you could travel to your destination in an ocean liner are over; these days people take to the air when they emigrate. The airline business is very competitive these days and it is worthwhile shopping around for the best deal — which could mean low fares, half-price fares for children, a generous luggage allowance, a free stop-over *en route* (in the case of Australia or New Zealand).

There are a growing number of travel agents around that specialise in discounted fares, though you should check that they are ABTA bonded before you part with any cash. A number of firms that claim expertise in arranging travel for migrants advertise in the migrant newspapers mentioned elsewhere in this book.

YOUR WILL

Whenever your circumstances change radically, it makes sense to look at your will and decide whether any modifications are necessary.

MAKING A CHECKLIST

The checklist (Fig. 6) should help to remind you of the matters you need to see to. Not all will be applicable to your circumstances, but you may have others to add to the list.

Notes
[1] *Brits Abroad*, Harry Brown & Rosemary Thomas (Express Books 1981).

Item	Notes
Bank	
Car	
Circulate new address	
Credit or charge card company	
Dentist	
Department of Social Security: notify new address; obtain form E112 (if appropriate)	
Disposal of surplus personal effects	
District council: pay Council Tax and any other dues	
Doctor: check-up; prescription	
Electricity: give at least 48 hours' notice	
Financial advice	
Gas: give at least 48 hours' notice	
Insurance	
Landlord (if a tenant): give notice according to terms of contract	
Library: return books	
Magazine subscriptions: cancel or have redirected	
Medical card: surrender to immigration official	
Milkman: cancel	
Newspapers deliveries: cancel	
Optician	
Pension administrator	
Passport	
Post Office: forwarding of mail	
Removal company	
Rental or HP agreements: terminate	
Savings: notify organisations of change of address (e.g. National Savings Office, Premium Bond Office, stockbroker, etc.)	
Solicitor	
Storage of personal effects	
Visa	
Telephone: Give at least 7 days' notice	
Transport of personal effects	
Travel arrangements	
Water company	

Fig. 6. Checklist: things to do before leaving.

7
Settling in Successfully

If you want people to think well of you, do not speak well of yourself. (Blaise Pascal)

You have spent the past months preparing your application and persuading migration service officials that you are a model migrant; you have wound up your affairs and prepared diligently for the future; you have dealt with removal firms, financial adviser, solicitors, estate agents, doctors, dentists, vets, insurance brokers — to name but a few.

And now you have arrived in the country you have set your heart on. Does this mean you can sit back, relax and drink in the atmosphere?

Certainly not. The settling-in period is a most crucial time when you have to keep your wits about you. You need to get acclimatised and established; this is a time when you lay the foundations of your new life.

If you are joining relations they will doubtless offer you support and encouragement as you adjust to life in a different climate amid different surroundings. Those who have used the services of a migration consultancy may find there is a local office which assists newly arrived immigrants. If not, there are often statutory bodies (e.g. Migrant Centres in Australia) or voluntary organisations (e.g. the 1820 Settlers Association in South Africa) which can help you find your feet.

ACCOMMODATION

Unless friends or relatives offer to put you up for a while, you will need temporary accommodation, and if you are travelling with a family you ought to reserve this in advance.

Hotel
This is a sensible option initially, but could work out expensive in the long term, particularly with a family. Some countries have less expensive apartment-type hotels suitable for long stays.

Guest house
These are less expensive than hotels and worth considering initially, but families might find them restrictive after a while.

Serviced flat
This might prove more convenient and work out less expensive, since you would enjoy greater independence, be able to prepare your own meals, and so on. A short- to medium-term option.

Migrant accommodation
Some governments (e.g. Australia) have special short-term accommodation for migrants when they arrive, and you might investigate the availability of this.

Rented furnished accommodation (flat or house)
The availability of furnished accommodation varies from place to place, and you might have to search high and low. It is worth considering as a medium-term measure if you are not bringing your own furniture into the country.

Rented unfurnished housing
If you are having a substantial amount of personal effects sent out, you need to find unfurnished accommodated when they arrive, to avoid the expense of storage. It is worth investing plenty of time searching for a place since it might be your home for months or years.

Your own home
Most migrants aim to become owner-occupiers. However, property purchase is not something to be rushed into, unless you have lived in the country before and know precisely what you are going to need. It is viable only when you have settled on a particular location and know that you are going to live there for some time. It is unlikely that you will recoup your initial outlay if you sell up within a couple of years.

Except in the larger cities where apartment accommodation is more common, you will find that the average house in the countries we are considering is detached and standing in its own grounds.

What to do about renting
You should make sure you have a written contract which sets out the rental you have to pay and the obligations of both tenant and landlord, including length of the lease and the amount of notice to be given to quit. In the case

of furnished accommodation there will be an inventory to check and sign. Normally you will have to pay a deposit which is refundable provided you leave the accommodation in good condition.

What to do about buying

As in the UK this is a major commitment and you need to work out whether the investment is worth it, as prices can fluctuate. If you are taking out a mortgage you may have to make a larger down-payment on the dwelling than in the UK and there may not be tax rebates. Purchasing costs may work out higher too. In South Africa, for instance, it is the purchaser who pays the house agent's commission (which could be as much as 6 per cent) and there will usually be stamp duty to pay as well.

Although you may be familiar with conveyancing in the UK, practice in other countries may differ in some respects. In Australia and South Africa, for instance, agreements are legally binding and completion dates fixed in advance. For this reason it is prudent to employ your own solicitor or attorney.

BANKING

The chances are that you will need to open a bank account if you have not already done so. You should ask around to find out which bank offers the best service and would be best suited to your needs.

It may take time for your account to get into gear and you will doubtless be required to provide references (e.g. from your employer or your bank in the UK) which have to be checked. Be prepared for differences in banking practice. In Australia, for instance, there are no bank guarantee cards, and the United States has no national bank networks as such.

CUSTOMS

With luck you will not have to pay duty on your personal effects, but expect a certain amount of red tape. If you are importing a car, you will usually have to pay duty before the vehicle is released from customs.

DRIVING

While in most countries you can drive on your British driving licence initially, sooner or later you need to obtain a local driving licence. In federal countries this is usually issued by the state or province in which

you are living, and you should enquire about this soon after your arrival.
You may be expected to take a driving test.

You should always make sure you are acquainted with the local
Highway Code, which may differ in some respects from UK regulations.
I stress 'local' since in Australia driving practice differs from state to state.

FINDING WORK

If you have taken the advice in Chapter 5 you may already have a job
arranged, or else you may have set proceedings in motion and secured a
number of interviews.

If not, your early days will be extremely busy. Relatively few immigrants have substantial reserves to live on, so finding a job is a first
priority. You will probably have to devote much of your time to the job
search. Disregard tales you hear of people who managed to walk into a
job on the day they arrived; they tend to be the exception. Indeed it would
be wise to budget for an extended job hunt lasting weeks or months.

One advantage of starting your job search *in situ* is that you will have
access to a full range of up-to-date publications containing job advertisements and will be able to respond to them immediately.

Yet waiting for the right advertisement to appear should be just one of
several job search methods you should pursue (see Chapter 5). Advertisements are not always the best means of finding a job, since they often
attract scores of applicants, most of whom will have lived in the country
all their lives. Being up against local talent could act to your disadvantage
in the eyes of the employer because

●   you have no experience of working in the country and they have
●   the referees you cite live overseas whereas they can offer referees
    who are more easily contactable.

For this reason your best plan might be to seize the initiative and adopt
a speculative approach. This involves sending copies of your CV with a
covering letter to a range of employers and recruitment agencies and
following it up with either a telephone call or a visit.

In many countries there are government employment agencies (e.g.
Canada Employment Centres and the Commonwealth Employment Service in Australia) and it is sensible to register with these and find out what
facilities they offer. Do not hesitate to make use of other contacts, such
as professional associations, chambers of commerce, or even your Great
Uncle Silas.

If despite your best efforts permanent job offers fail to materialise, you should consider taking a temporary position. There are temporary staff agencies in most countries and they often deal with a range of jobs, not just secretarial ones. Apart from providing much needed cash some temporary jobs can develop into permanent positions. Even if yours does not, you are gaining valuable experience of the work set-up which will put you in a stronger position when you next apply for a permanent post.

The Appendix offers a few suggestions as to how you might present yourself to potential employers.

GETTING TO KNOW THE PEOPLE

If you are joining your family or have friends in your adopted country, you have a ready-made entrée into local society. They will introduce you to people, the way of life and may even have suggestions regarding job opportunities.

If you are an independent immigrant you may find the going harder particularly if you are of a shy disposition. Yet there may be help close at hand. As mentioned at the beginning of the chapter, some governments provide support facilities for migrants (e.g. the South Australian Migration Service) to help you over the early stages. Such assistance may also be provided by voluntary bodies (e.g. the 1820 Settlers Association of South Africa), local churches or expatriate societies. There are, for instance, St Andrew's societies all over the world to serve the needs of the Scots.

However, sometimes the initiative needs to come from you, and you need to go out of your way to cultivate people at the outset. Join clubs (both social and professional), socialise with your workmates (when you get a job), and be prepared to lend a helping hand when needed.

Even though the locals speak English and look like you there may be differences of attitudes or approach, and you need to get accustomed to this. If you can't beat 'em, join 'em. You will win more friends if you are positive about the country and its institutions than if you are prone to criticise and carp.

HEALTH CARE

In countries where there is a state health-care system it is essential to register with this even if you have plans to take out private medical insurance. Where there is no universal health-care system (in South

Africa, the USA) you should make sure you have adequate private cover. This is often provided by the employer.

Whether you are covered by private or state insurance you will find that certain forms of cover are excluded, notably dental treatment, opticians — and even the ambulance service in Australia. In such cases you should consider taking out private insurance.

HOMESICKNESS

There will be times when you will have second thoughts about emigration and feel terribly homesick. You miss your relations and friends, familiar places and familiar routines. Your adopted country seems strange and forbidding; it does not feel a bit like home. You contemplate going back.

Homesickness is often a consequence of culture shock. In theory Westerners should have little difficulty in coming to terms with another predominantly Western society, but there will be subtle differences that may bother you. People from a different culture whose mother tongue is not English are likely to experience much greater difficulty in coming to grips with a new situation.

Yet thanks to modern technology, home is not very far away. International telephone calls are infinitely cheaper in real terms than they used to be, and the cost is likely to come down even more. Nevertheless, they remain an expensive way of keeping in touch. Keeping in touch by letter is cheaper and often more effective in keeping relationships alive; or if you want to be really up-to-date why not send audio-cassettes and video-cassettes of yourself to your family and friends.

If you find that there is little coverage of the UK in the local media, you can compensate by acquiring a radio with a short waveband and tune into the BBC World Service. In some parts of the world you can also receive BBC television programmes by satellite, and you should contact the BBC at Bush House for further details.

You may discover it to be prohibitively expensive to buy British daily newspapers regularly, but there are some weeklies you might consider subscribing to (e.g. the *Guardian Weekly,* the *Weekly Telegraph, The Economist.*)

MAILING ADDRESS

Once you get a permanent address you need to advise your friends, relations and professional advisers.

REGISTRATION

Soon after you arrive you will need to register with a number of organisations, notably the tax authorities and the social security office, who will issue you with an identification number which you may have to produce for potential employers or if you are opening a bank account.

As long as you remain a British citizen, you ought to register with the nearest British Consul — other nationalities should contact their respective diplomatic missions. The Consul will be able to supply you with a list of local contacts and electoral forms enabling you to vote in a British election. There may be occasions in the future when you will need to apply to him or her for assistance and advice, particularly of a legal nature. You may even receive an invitation to celebrate the Queen's Birthday at some future date.

SCHOOLING

If you have children of school age, you will need to enrol them at some educational establishment. Educational arrangements for your offspring are dealt with at length in Chapter 6, and you may well have started the process.

If not, you will need to ask around to discover which schools are best suited to your children, and this is particularly crucial at the secondary stage. Local educational departments can provide you with a list of state schools and offer advice, and directories of private schools are usually obtainable from libraries or from the relevant association of private schools.

A change of school can pose problems of adjustment for some children, particularly if the teaching methods and the syllabus differ from the UK, and they will need all the support and encouragement you can muster. Ideally your child should start school at the beginning of the school year, which is February in Australia and New Zealand.

STARTING WORK

Your first day in a new job can be a bewildering experience, even more so if you are starting work in a new country. With luck, however, you will be offered some form of induction or someone will take you under their wing. You should never refuse offers of help and should always be prepared to ask questions.

Make sure that you get a contract, and that you read through the terms carefully. In the US, for instance, the contract is an important document if you ever need to seek legal redress against your employer.

Work practices differ from country to country, and you should take nothing for granted. People in the United States and Canada, for instance, tend to be hard-working, and it is simply not done to turn up late for work or leave early. Even if you hold a fairly senior position you may have to clock on and clock off.

While you may have your own ideas as to how things should be done, you should endeavour to accommodate yourself to the practices of the organisation — at least until you know the ropes. Australia, for instance, is strongly unionised, and you might risk a demarkation dispute if you ask an employee to undertake work which he or she is not contracted to do.

TAXATION

Once you become a resident of a country you become liable for taxation, and one of the first things you may need to do is register with the tax authorities. In federal countries, such as Australia, Canada and the USA, taxes are levied by the federal government, the state government, and sometimes by the local council as well. In Australia, for instance, the federal government collects income tax; the state governments collect stamp duty, petrol and payroll taxes; and real estate taxes are collected by local councils.

Usually the tax authorities catch up with you in the end, but there may well be a legal obligation on your part to register with them.

UTILITIES

Sooner or later you will have dealings with telephone, electricity, gas and water companies. You should find out in advance if you will need to pay a connection charge or a deposit, and if so, how much.

8
Australia

Do you know, Mr Hopper, dear Agatha and I are so much interested in Australia. It must be so pretty with dear little kangaroos flying about. (Oscar Wilde, *Lady Windermere's Fan*.)[1]

Its worst faults are aggressiveness which leads easily to violence in word and deed, and a dreadful complacency; its greatest virtues courage and a certain downright honesty which at least says what it thinks. (John Douglas Pringle, *Australian Accent*.)[2]

Australia is a continent which is almost as large as the USA (excluding Alaska and Hawaii), and 25 times the size of the British Isles. Yet compared with its area of 2,967,909 square miles (7,682,300 sq. km) its population is tiny — only 18 million. This works out at roughly two people per square kilometre.

Distances are enormous: Sydney is over 2,000 miles east of Perth; Darwin is nearly 2,400 miles from Hobart, and there are hardly any sizeable settlements in between except for Alice Springs. 'This country is a rim containing people round a withered hub', notes Elspeth Huxley.[3] Much of the interior is empty; virtually everyone lives on the perimeter — the majority in the south-eastern corner.

It is important to dissociate reality from myth. Australia is not a nation of rugged sheep farmers and miners who keep their women in their place and guzzle vast quantities of beer. Around two-thirds of the population live not in the outback but in the eight capital cities of the various states and territories. In fact, Australians make up one of the most urbanised societies in the world.

Thanks to the climate there is plenty of emphasis on the outdoor life in the form of sailing, wind surfing, racing, cricket, football (including Australian rules football) and outdoor barbecues. However, the country also has a well-developed arts and entertainment scene — with a buoyant film industry, opera and ballet companies, symphony orchestras and sophisticated night life. There is an impressive variety of restaurants in

93

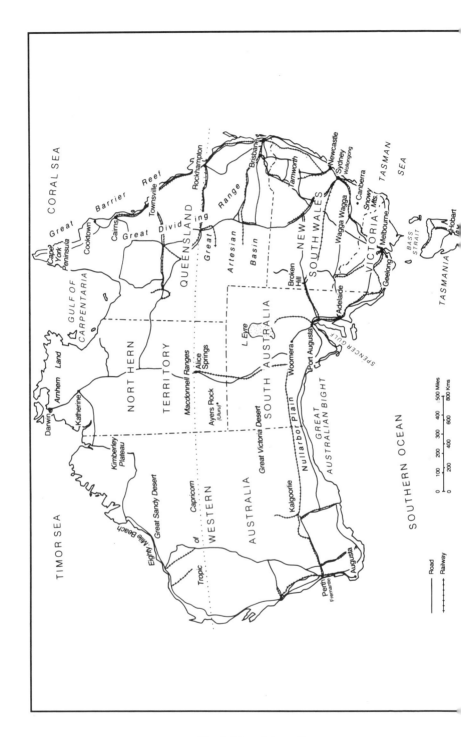

Fig. 7. Map of Australia

94

all the main centres and Australian wines have acquired a reputation for quality.

Although supposedly a very egalitarian society with a strong trade union movement, there is some social differentiation and people tend to be judged by what they own, what they earn and where they live. The country's ties with Britain have become more tenuous as it has drawn closer to the other countries of the Pacific rim, and there are moves afoot to make the country a republic.

While Australia may once have been a dumping ground for misfits and ne'er-do-wells, the rough diamond image is becoming a thing of the past. Indeed the younger generation of Australians are for the most part sophisticated and widely travelled.

STATES

Australia is a federation of states and territories which came together in 1901 to form the Commonwealth of Australia. The individual states have a good deal of autonomy, and most of them have their own offices in London and elsewhere, which are an excellent source of information.

New South Wales
Population: 6 million; *area:* 309,433 sq. miles/801,427 sq. km; *capital:* Sydney (3.5 million); *other cities:* Newcastle (420,000); Wollongong (235,000)
The most heavily populated state and the major business and financial centre. It produces the bulk of the country's steel, rice and cotton. One-third of the population lives in this south-eastern corner of the continent which is rated as having very good long-term growth prospects. The coastal zone is a favourite retirement area.

Sydney is Australia's oldest and largest city with an atmosphere not unlike New York. Other Australians regard Sydney residents as brash and lacking in good taste, but it may be a case of sour grapes. Like all large cities it suffers from expensive housing, congestion and long journeys to work. It is likely to expand even further in the next few years now that it is to host the 2000 Olympic Games.

Queensland
Population: 3 million; *area:* 666,798 sq. miles/1,727,00 sq. km; *capital:* Brisbane (1.25 million)
More than 50 per cent of Australia's second largest state lies within the tropics and Queensland is sometimes compared to the American 'Deep

South'. Tourism is a major industry and it has become a favourite holiday and retirement location. Mining and agriculture are also very important and the state is regarded as the most prosperous in the country with good growth prospects. The state is popular with immigrants from the UK because of its climate.

Brisbane, the country's third largest city, has a more informal lifestyle than other state capitals. Daily temperatures rarely drop below 70 degrees(F) even in the winter.

South Australia
Population: 1.5 million; *area:* 380,070 sq. miles/984,376 sq. km; *capital:* Adelaide (1 million)
This state appears very keen to attract immigrants, and its Immigrant Promotion Unit provides back-up on their arrival. It is a centre for the Australian wine industry and an important manufacturing base. Mining is also important.

Adelaide is Australia's fourth largest city and its biennial Festival of Arts the country's largest cultural event. It enjoys a Mediterranean climate, has a more relaxed atmosphere than Sydney and Melbourne, and is also less expensive and congested.

Tasmania
Population: 470,000; *area:* 26,383 sq. miles/68,331 sq. km; *capital:* Hobart (180,000)
The smallest and least urbanised state in the country is some distance from the mainland and boasts the country's second oldest capital city. Agriculture, fishing and forestry play an important role in the economy. There is an abundance of natural resources and the people are very environmentally conscious. Job opportunities, however, are limited.

Victoria
Population: 4.5 million; *area:* 87.876 sq. miles/227,597 sq. km; *capital:* Melbourne (3 million); *other cities:* Geelong (150,000)
The state is responsible for one-third of Australia's industrial output, including motor manufacturing, chemicals, electronics, clothing and footwear and textiles. The eastern part is very fertile while the north-west tends to be warm and dry.

Melbourne has a more British feel than Sydney; perhaps the unpredictable weather has something to do with it. The country's largest port and an important business and financial centre, it has many picturesque nineteenth-century buildings, large parks and trams. It also sprawls over an area twice the size of London.

Western Australia
Population: 1.7 million; *area:* 975,920 sq. miles/2,527,621 sq. km; *capital:* Perth (1.12 million)

The country's largest state, accounting for one-third of the area of Australia, currently attracts the largest number of migrants from Britain. The northern part is tropical while the south has a pleasant Mediterranean climate. Its abundant mineral resources should ensure continued prosperity for the state.

Much of the population lives in the Perth region, which is an important industrial centre and boasts a symphony orchestra, opera and ballet company. Western Australia is remote from the rest of Australia and is developing close relationships with South East Asia.

TERRITORIES

Northern Territory
Population: 170,000; *area:* 520,280 sq. miles *capital:* Darwin
More than 80 per cent of this sparsely populated state lies within the tropics and gets very hot in summer. Mining and tourism are the major industries. On average the population is younger than elsewhere in the country and many are working on short-term contracts.

This sounds ideal territory for a frontiersman with events like Darwin Beer Can Regatta using boats made of beer cans and Henley on Todd Regatta at Alice Springs where the boats have no bottoms and the river has no water.

Australian Capital Territory
Population: 300,000; *area:* 939 sq. miles; *capital:* Canberra
Canberra was chosen as the Federal Capital as long ago as 1909, and the Australian parliament moved here in 1927. Most of the development has occurred since the war. Around 60 per cent of the workforce are civil servants — so migrants are unlikely to make for Canberra in the first instance. The area has a high population growth rate but little industry.

LIVING IN AUSTRALIA

In the media Australians appear affable, sociable people, but their cheerful disposition may hide an uncertain interior. 'There is a sense of isolation and although the ''tyranny of distance'' is less of a problem it is still there, at least in the minds of most people,' notes JC.

Clearly the tough recession has had a profound effect on people who have come to realise they can no longer 'live off the sheep's back'. 'My (Australian) fiancé was horrified about how things had changed in a matter of years,' reports HN. 'He found the people rather difficult, lacking in humour and with a chip on their shoulders.'

She found the scenery of Western Australia compensated partly for the drawbacks. There are also good benefits for employees including ten days' official sick leave which everyone is expected to take, though employers expect high standards.

Properties are cheap in that state with rentals less than half those in the UK. GI points to a number of other advantages: 'Perth is more of a beach resort than a city; there is no congestion thanks to good town planning, and no pollution either.' It is particularly popular with middle-aged immigrants. He is also impressed with the school facilities.

For Australia as a whole, JC notes that the standard of living has fallen and wages and salaries are much lower than in Europe. 'You get less choice of consumer and other goods, the clothes are poor quality and expensive and there is a trend towards US culture.'

IMMIGRATION PROSPECTS

Over 4 million people from 120 countries have settled in Australia since the Second World War. Britain remains the largest single source of immigrants — there are 700,000 British migrants in the workforce, or around 10 per cent of the total. Italians and Greeks have made their mark, and more recently so have the Chinese, Vietnamese, Filipinos, Turks and Lebanese.

However unlimited immigration is now a thing of the past. Australia has been badly hit by the world recession, and at the time of writing unemployment is hovering around 11 per cent in much of Australia. Pay is lower than Western European levels. Clearly the economy is not in a position to absorb a large influx of immigrants at present.

In the 1993 General Election the opposition Liberal-National Party advocated suspending immigration, but it lost. The Labour Government is committed to admitting immigrants and in 1993 the quota of permanent residence visas stood at 80,000. This figure is subject to modification in future years, and much will depend on how quickly the Australian economy revives.

IMMIGRATION CHECKLIST

If you work through the following questions you will be able to assess your eligibility for an immigrant visa.

1. Have you a relation who is either an Australian citizen or an Australian resident who is prepared to sponsor you? Sponsorship involves assisting financially and with respect to accommodation during your first twelve months

    YES   Go to 2.
    NO   Go to 4. (If you wish to retire to Australia go to 9.)

2. Does your relationship to the sponsor fall into one of the following categories?

    ●   spouse (or *de facto* partner) of the sponsor

    ●   fiancé(e) of the sponsor

    ●   unmarried or dependent child of your sponsor and not married or engaged

    ●   a child under 18 adopted overseas or for adoption in Australia

    ●   parent of your sponsor who meets the 'balance of family' test (i.e. at least half their children live in Australia)

    ●   unmarried orphan under 18 years old related to the sponsor

    ●   a relative capable of providing substantial continuing assistance to a sponsor in need of permanent or long-term assistance

    ●   an elderly unmarried relative financially dependent on the sponsor

    ●   your sponsor's last remaining relative overseas (brother, sister or non-dependent child).

    YES   You come under the Preferential Family Migration Programme.
    NO   Go to 3.

3. Does your relationship to the sponsor fall into one of the following categories?

    ● non-dependent child

    ● a parent of working age who does not pass the 'balance of family' test

    ● a brother or sister

    ● a niece or nephew.

    YES You qualify for the Concessional Family Migration Programme and if you pass the 'points test' (see below). If you do not have the requisite minimum number of points, your application is likely to be turned down. Go to 4.
    NO   Go to 4

4. Don't despair. You may qualify for a migrant visa under the Skill Migration Programme.

    Are you under 55 and nominated by an employer within the framework of a labour agreement?

    YES You are eligible for a Class 120 Labour Agreement visa.
    NO   Go to 5.

5. Are you under 55 and nominated for a job vacancy which cannot be filled from the Australian workforce?

    YES You are eligible for a Class 121 Employer Nomination Scheme visa.
    NO   Go to 6.

6. Have you distinguished yourself internationally in the arts or sport?

    YES You may be eligible for a Class 124 or 125 Distinguished Talent visa.
    NO   Go to 7.

7. Are you a highly skilled person whose education, skills and ready
    employability will contribute to the Australian economy?

    YES   If you think you are, refer to the points test (see below). If you
    have the required minimum number of points (currently 110) you can
    qualify as an Independent Entrant. If you fail the test, go to 8.
    NO   Go to 8.

8. Are you a successful business person (shareholder, sole proprietor,
    senior executive) intending to establish a business venture in Austra-
    lia?

    YES   Assess your eligibility by doing the business skills test. If you
    do not score the requisite number of points (currently 105), you may
    still qualify, but you should seek professional advice.
    NO   Go to 9.

9. You may not be able to work in Australia, but you may still be able
    to retire to Australia — sooner or later. However, you need to
    demonstrate that you have a substantial amount of capital.

Note that there are also special immigrant programmes for refugees and
displaced persons. Temporary non-residence visas are available for business people, skilled people with job offers, and under-25s.

THE POINTS TEST

For a Concessional Family visa or an Independent Entrant visa you have
to refer to a table to work out your points score (see Fig. 8).

The Concessional Family visa takes account of:

●   your employability skills (qualifications and age)

●   your relationship to your sponsor

●   the length of time your sponsor has been an Australian citizen (if at
    all)

●   whether your sponsor has been resident in Australia and employed
    for the past two years.

Points table for people interested in emigrating to Australia.

The pool entrance marks will be 90 points for Concessional Family and 100 points for Independent migrants. The Priority and pass mark will be 100 points for Concessional Family and 110 points for Independent migrants.

Concessional Family visa class applicants may score points for Skill, Age, Relationship, Citizenship, Settlement and Location. They are *not* scored on the Language Skills factor.
Independent Entrant visa class applicants may only score points for Skill, Age and Language Skills.
Proficiency in English is an additional mandatory requirement for *any* principal application whose usual occupation (i) is on the Occupations Requiring English (ORE) list.

Employability Factor
Skill sub-factor
The qualifications and experience listed in this factor relate to the qualifications and experience needed to work in the usual occupation (i) in Australia.
Qualifications will be examined by the appropriate assessing authority. To achieve the points set out below, the qualifications
— must be assessed as equivalent to the Australian qualification level listed below; and
— must be relevant to the usual occupation.

Occupations which in Australia require:

Trade cert/degree (acceptable), with at least 3 years post-qualification work experience	70
Trade cert/degree (acceptable), with between 6 months and 3 years post-qualification work experience	60
Diploma (acceptable), with at least 3 years post-qualification work experience	55
Diploma (acceptable), with between 6 months and 3 years post-qualification work experience	50
Trade cert/degree/diploma (recognised overseas and assessed by Australian authorities as requiring only minor upgrading), with at least 3 years post-qualification work experience	30
Post secondary school qualifications	25
Trade cert/degree/diploma but qualifications held are unacceptable	25
12 years of primary and secondary education	20
10 years of primary and secondary education	10
Less than 10 years education	0

Fig. 8. Points table for emigration to Australia.

Age sub-factor
18 to 29 years	30
30 to 34 years	20
35 to 39 years	10
40 to 49 years	5
50 years plus/less than 18 years	0

Language skills sub-factor
Proficient in English	20
Reasonably proficient English but minor training required	10
Bilingual in languages other than English, or only limited English ability	5
Extensive English training required	0

Independent migrants only

Family relationship factor
Relationship of applicant to sponsor:
Parent	15
Brother, sister, non-dependent child	10
Nephew or niece	5

Citizenship factor
If the sponsor has been an:
Australian citizen for 5 years or more	10
Australian citizen for less than 5 years	5

Settlement factor
If your sponsor, or the spouse of the sponsor, has been in continuous employment in Australia for the last two years (no unemployment, special benefits for more than four weeks in total) and is not currently in receipt of any form of Social Security Benefit, Allowance or Pension other than the Age or War Veterans pension — 10

Location factor
If the sponsor has lived in a State/Territory designated area for the last two years — 5

Concessional migrants — *Family only*

Note: Usual occupation is a job in which the applicant has worked for a continuous period of six months during a two-year period immediately preceding the application. If the applicant's usual occupation is as a medical practitioner a 10 point skill factor penalty will apply.

Fig. 8. Continued.

Factor 1 — Business Attributes

	Points Score
Shareholders/sole proprietors:	
The principal business had an annual turnover of not less than the amount specified below in not less than 2 of the 3 years preceding the application:	
–$A 5,000,000; and	
–the major activity was in a designated industry sector	75
–$A 3,000,000; and	
–the major activity was in a designated industry sector	70
–$A 1,500,000; and	
–the major activity was in a designated industry sector	65
–$A 750,000; and	
–employed not less than 5 full time employees and	60
–$A 5,000,000; and	
–employed not less than 5 full time employees; and	60
–$A 500,000;	
–employed not less than 5 full time employees; and	55
–the major activity was in a designated industry sector	
–$A 3,000,000; and	
–employed not less than 5 full time employees	55
–$A 1,500,000; and	
–employed not less than 5 full time employees	50
–$A 750,000; and	
–employed not less than 5 full time employees	40
–$A 500,000; and	
–employed not less than 5 full time employees	35
Senior Executive in a major business where:	
–the major activity is in a designated industry sector	65
–the major activity is not in a designated industry sector	60

Note: the 'Designated Industry Sectors List' for the purpose of the above is to comprise manufacturing, traded services and development and use of innovative technologies.

Details of designated industry sectors will be published in the Commonwealth Gazette before the commencement of the new category.

Fig. 9. Business skills test for emigration to Australia.

Factor 2 — Age

At the time of application the applicant is aged	Point Score
Not less than 30 years but under 45 years	30
Not less than 45 years but under 50 years	20
Not less than 25 years but under 30 years	15
Not less than 50 years but under 56 years	10
Less than 25 or more than 55 years	0

Factor 3 – Language

The Applicant has	Point Score
High ability to read, write and speak English	30
Moderate ability to read, write and speak English	20
High ability to read, write and speak in two or more languages other than English and has enrolment in a designated English course before entry to Australia	10
Low ability to read, write and speak English and has enrolment in a designated English course before entry to Australia	10
Low or no ability to read, write and speak English	0

Note: designated English courses and the institutions offering them will be published in the Commonwealth Gazette before the commencement of the new category.

Factor 4 — Capital

Net assets of applicant and spouse	Point Score
Not less than $A 2,500,000	15
Not less than $A 1,500,000 but less than $A 2,500,000	10
Not less than $A 500,000 but less than $A 1,500,000	5
Less than $A 500,000	0

The application fee for the Business Skills category will be $1,600.

Fig. 9. Continued.

• whether your sponsor has lived in a designated area for the last two years. (Most parts of Australia are currently designated areas, apart from New South Wales, Melbourne, Perth, Brisbane and the Sunshine and Gold Coasts.)

The Independent Entrant Visa takes account of

• your employability skills (qualifications and age)

• your language skills. If you speak English you score the maximum mark.

The number of points required to qualify for a visa varies from year to year depending on the number of employment opportunities. In 1992/93 the number of Concessionary Family visas was limited to 6,000 and the number of Independent Entrants to 12,000.

In 1993 100 points were needed for a Concessional Family visa and 110 for an Independent Entrant visa. The pool entry mark was 90 points and 100 points respectively. There were no priority occupations.

You may be required to have your skills or qualifications assessed to see how they measure up to Australian standards as set down by the National Overseas Office of Skills Recognition. The High Commission in the UK has staff who are able to conduct assessments for most occupations.

In 1993 the number of points needed to qualify was 105. Designated state and territory agencies can offer sponsorship to businesses which they consider will make a particular contribution to the local economy. This gives a business owner an additional 15 points under the business skills migration test and reduces his minimum net assets requirement from $350,000 to $200,000 (see Fig. 9).

THE ROLE OF THE SPONSOR

In addition to providing assistance and accommodation to migrants for their first year in Australia, they will also be required to undertake a legal commitment (Assurance of Support) to repay any social security or health costs incurred during the first two years. In many cases the sponsor has to lodge a refundable bond with an approved financial institution and pay a health service charge. In 1993 the bond amounted to A$3,500 and the health charge A$822.

DRIVING

Issue of driving licences is the responsibility of the individual states. Procedures for acquiring them differ and you may need to pass a driving test. The rules of the road differ slightly from state to state.

EDUCATION

The school year starts in February and education is compulsory from the age of six, though some children start earlier or attend pre-school kindergartens. The structure of education differs slightly from state to state.

In most states children aged 6–12 attend primary school (years 1–7); from 13–17 they attend secondary school (years 8–12) where they take school certificate in the 10th year, and higher school certificate in the 12th year. (In Western Australia this is called the certificate of secondary education; and in Adelaide the matriculation certificate.)

In addition to the state schools Australia boasts a wide range of private schools. These tend to be day schools and are run by religious bodies. Correspondence schools and the School of the Air cater for pupils in remote areas. Tertiary education in Australia is highly regarded and student grants may be forthcoming.

TAXATION

On arrival in Australia you will need to lodge an application with the Taxation Office in order to obtain a personal tax file number. You will need to disclose this to your employer and bank (or other financial institution in which you have an account that earns interest). Failure to do so will result in deductions being made at the highest marginal rate of tax.

SOCIAL SECURITY

The UK has a limited social security agreement with Australia which is detailed in Leaflet SA5. The benefits covered by the agreement are sickness benefit, age pension and widows benefit.

National Health insurance is funded through a levy on taxable income, and covers hospitalisation and 85 per cent of the fee charged by GPs, specialists and optometrists. Dental care, eye treatment, physiotherapy and ambulance service have to be insured through private health benefit organisations. Migrants should register as soon as they arrive by completing an application form at any Medicare office.

Employers contribute towards a pension on behalf of their employees.

Year	Jun 94	Dec 94	Jun 95	Dec 95	Jun 96	Dec 96
Sydney	195,400	203,400	211,800	215,400	214,700	212,600
Melbourne	143,800	147,800	152,300	155,800	159,300	162,800
Brisbane	153,300	154,900	155,200	156,400	159,500	161,400
Perth	117,100	122,500	127,200	125,900	125,800	125,100
Adelaide	123,800	122,800	126,500	129,000	127,100	124,400
Canberra	156,500	159,600	160,500	161,700	162,000	163,700
Hobart	101,800	105,500	109,500	104,900	105,400	109,100
Darwin	128,750	130,700	133,300	133,000	134,600	135,000

Source: Real Estate Institute of Australia.

Fig. 10. Projected house prices in Australia, 1994–6 (Australian dollars).

	Starting salaries for graduates	*Average earnings*
NSW	$26,000	$30,800
ACT	$25,000	$29,800
Victoria	$25,100	$28,600
SA	£25,000	$31,300
WA	$24,000	$28,200
Tas	$24,700	$31,500
NT	$26,500	$33,300

Source: Graduate Careers Council of Australia.

Fig. 11. Average salaries in Australia, 1991.

1	Brisbane	6	Melbourne
2	Canberra-Queanbeyan	7	Gold Coast-Tweed Heads
3	Sydney	8	Toowoomba
4	Adelaide	9	Sunshine Coast
5	Perth	10	Townsville

Source: Personal Investment Magazine.

Fig. 12. Most liveable and comfortable city in Australia (out of 20), 1993 (based on level of medical services, housing affordability, average wages, crime rates, pollution, unemployment and the financial strength of the state government).

HOUSE PURCHASE

Seventy per cent of homes in Australia are owner-occupied and most of these are detached bungalows standing in their own grounds (they are not called 'bungalows' by Australians). House purchasers normally scan the housing ads in the Saturday morning newspapers, enlist the services of an estate agent who is registered with the Real Estate Institute or bid at auctions. Mortgages are obtainable from banks (which may also undertake conveyancing) and building societies. Projected prices in Australia for the next three years are shown in Fig. 10. Conveyancing follows British practice with a 'subject to finance' clause in the contract.

JOB-FINDING

The Department of Employment, Education and Training offers assistance and advice to job-seekers and would-be entrepreneurs on broadly similar lines to those on offer in Britain, albeit with different titles.

The Commonwealth Employment Service
This handles job vacancies at all levels, and there are private recruitment consultants in most cities (listed under Employment Agencies in *Yellow Pages*).

Careers Reference Centres
These occupational information libraries are located in most large cities and are listed in telephone directories.

UK-based organisations
Among those that can provide information and assistance are Jobsearch, LEADS and Walker & Walker.

Salaries
Average salaries for 1991 are given in Fig. 11.

MIGRATION CONSULTANTS

Australian Immigration Services, BCL Immigration Services, The Hartford Consultancy.

FURTHER INFORMATION

Australia House can provide you with some literature, including *Living in Australia* and *Welcome to Australia*, an information pack produced by the Department of Immigration, Local Government and Ethnic Affairs. The pack includes a useful booklet of contact addresses.

It would also be worth while to visit the office of the state in which you wish to reside which should be able to provide you with more specific details.

The monthly newspapers *Australian News* and *Australian Outlook* contain up-to-date details on prices, immigration requirements and the state of the economy as well as location profiles (see also Fig. 12 which lists the most liveable and comfortable cities in 1993).

Consyl Publishing distribute a number of Australian magazines and annuals which would be of interest to the migrant. They include the *Houses for Sale* series for different Australian cities, *Owners Own* (houses and businesses for sale), *Businesses for Sale, New Car Guide, Choosing a School* series (various states), *Complete Retirement Guide* (various states), *Tax Guide* (Australian Taxation Office).

There are a number of handbooks dealing with Australia (see Bibliography).

Notes
[1] *Lady Windermere's Fan*, Oscar Wilde (1892).
[2] *Australian Accent*, John Douglas Pringle (1958).
[3] *Their Shining Eldorado*, Elspeth Huxley (1967).

9
Canada

Years ago the British critic Ron Bryden said to me, 'Canadians are nice, very nice, and they expect everybody else to be very nice'; and I have yet to come up with a better definition. (Mordecai Richler, Canadian novelist)

Canada is really two countries held together by three nation saving bywords — conservatism, caution and compromise — bequeathed to us by Britain. (William Toye)

Canada with its 3,849,646 sq. miles (9,970,000 sq. km) is the second largest country in the world (after Russia) but is home to a comparatively modest 27 million people, ranking it 31st in the world in terms of population. Vast areas of the territory are uninhabited (or uninhabitable) and around 80 per cent of Canadians live in urban areas within 180 miles (300 km) of the border with the United States. In fact, 60 per cent are concentrated in the south of Ontario and Quebec.

Although Canada shares a continent with the United States, Canadians jealously guard their own identity. The country has a decentralised system of government with the administrations of the different provinces and territories largely responsible for their own affairs, including health care. The parliamentary and legal systems are closer to those of the UK than the USA, though Quebec law is closer to the French system.

Canada was originally a French settlement following Jacques Cartier's landing on the Caspe peninsula in 1534, and the population remained predominantly French until 1760. The situation changed when Britain established control in 1774 and there was a large influx of immigrants from Britain and the newly independent United States of America.

The majority of the population is still of British or French descent, and French and English continue to be Canada's official languages. However in this century a growing proportion of immigrants have come from other European countries and other parts of the world. A policy of multi-culturalism encourages ethnic minority groups to retain their own cultural heritage.

111

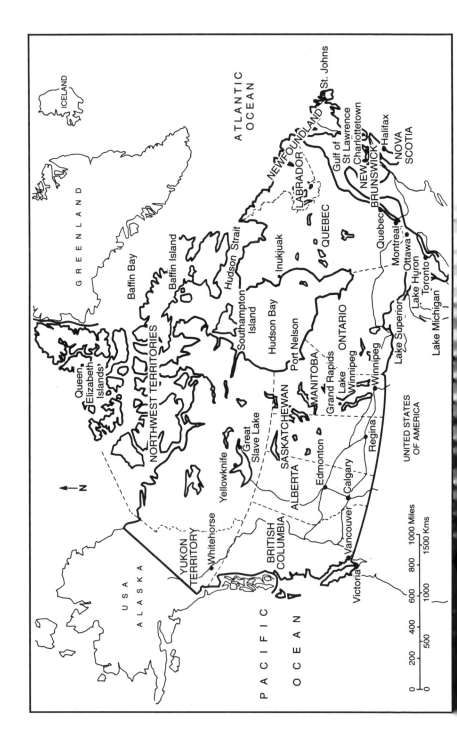

Fig. 13. Map of Canada

112

When RS became a Canadian citizen some years ago he took part in a ceremony where he swore allegiance to the country. 'The 42 people who took the oath with me came from no fewer than 42 different countries,' he says. 'That I think is the measure of how multi-cultural Canada is.'

Since the country covers such a vast area, the different areas of Canada have evolved a character of their own. British Columbia is British in character as well as in name. The Prairie Provinces seem more closely related to the American states south of the border. The Atlantic provinces have an English and Scottish feel.

The province of Quebec is more akin to France and continental Europe and differs quite markedly in traditions and procedures from the rest of Canada. Quebec Province may feel like a separate country in everything but name, while Montreal is the second largest French-speaking city in the world after Paris. Canada's richest province is Ontario which is also an important manufacturing centre.

The country is abundant in natural resources — notably forestry, agriculture and mining. However manufacturing and services are playing an increasingly important role in the economy now, particularly in the hi-tech field. While Canada welcomes immigrants, they now need to possess skills that are in demand.

THE REGIONS OF CANADA

Atlantic Canada
The economies of this area are still predominantly resource-based, not-ably agriculture, forestry and fishing. Temperatures are not as extreme as in the interior of the country. Newfoundland has the distinction of being Britain's first colony, and its capital, St John's, the oldest city in North America.

Newfoundland and Labrador
Population: 570,000; *area:* 156,649 sq. miles/405, 718 sq. km; *capital:* St John's (162,000)

Nova Scotia
Population: 900,000; *area:* 21,425 sq. miles/55,490 sq. km; *capital:* Halifax (180,000)

Prince Edward Island
Population: 130,000; *area:* 2,185 sq. miles/5,659 sq. km; *capital:*
Charlottetown (15,776)
Canada's smallest province.

New Brunswick
Population: 725,000; *area:* 28,355 sq. miles/73,439 sq. km; *capital:*
Fredericton (65,000); *Cities:* Saint John (121,000); Moncton (102,000)

Central Canada

The expression is something of a misnomer. Ontario and Quebec lie in
the eastern half of Canada and account for 60 per cent of the country's
population. The Great Lakes and the St Lawrence River have a moderating
effect on the winter temperatures in the southern part. Mining and forestry
remain important, but both provinces have strong manufacturing and
mining sectors. Indeed, around 75 per cent of Canada's manufactures
emanate from here.

Quebec
Population: 6.9 million; *area:* 594,855 sq. miles/1,540,667 sq. km; *capital:* Quebec City (350,000); *Cities:* Montreal (1 million); Laval (285,000)
With its French traditions Quebec stands apart from Canada's other
provinces and does its own immigrant selection. A knowledge of French
is really a must if you intend to settle here, and normally new immigrants
are expected to send their children to schools where French is the medium
of instruction. The issue of Quebec separatism raises its head from time
to time, but according to DW the province boasts a hard core of English
speaking people who are very pro-Quebec and are very content there.
Quebec has an office in London.

Ontario
Population: 10 million; *area:* 412,578 sq. miles/1,068,572 sq. km; *capital:* Toronto (2.2 million) Federal Capital: Ottawa (300,000); Hamilton:
(306,140); London (270,000)
Ethnically a very diverse province. Though the northern part is sparsely
populated, it accounts for one half of the country's manufacturing output
and is also an important producer of nickel, copper, uranium, gold and
zinc. One in four immigrants makes for Toronto, Canada's largest city,
which boasts a lively cosmopolitan atmosphere. There are said to be more
Italians living here than in any city outside Italy. Yet, unlike many other

cities of similar size it is clean and orderly and runs an efficient public
transport system.

The Prairies

The three Prairie Provinces did not really attract many settlers until the
construction of the Canadian Pacific Railway which united Canada for
the first time, and of those that made their homes here a large proportion
were from Central and Eastern Europe. This region boasts the most
ethnically diverse population, with no particular ethnic group predomi-
nating. The climate is continental with short, warm summers and long,
cold winters where temperatures can reach -40° (Fahrenheit). Mining and
agriculture are the mainstays of the economy. In fact, Alberta with its oil
and gas industry accounts for half the minerals produced in Canada by
value.

Manitoba
Population: 1,100,000; *area:* 250,745 sq. miles/649,426 sq. km; *capital:*
Winnipeg (600,000)

Saskatchewan
Population: 1 million; *area:* 251, 864 sq. miles/ 652, 324 sq. km; *capital:*
Regina (190,000); *other cities:* Saskatoon (205,000).
Office in London

Alberta
Population: 2,5 million; *area:* 255,285 sq. miles/661,185 sq. km; *capital:*
Edmonton 785,000; *other cities:* Calgary: (660,000)
Office in London

The west coast

The coastal strip is sometimes known as Lotus Land because of its climate:
with its mild wet winters and warm summers it has the longest frost-free
season in the whole of Canada. The recent influx of Hong Kong Chinese
has boosted house prices and given a fillip to the economy.

British Columbia
Population: 3.3 million; *area:* 365,944 sq. miles/947, 790 sq. km
Canada's third largest province. Half the population live in or around
Vancouver (1,455,000) and the provincial capital, Victoria (267,000). It
boasts the most beautiful scenery of all Canada's provinces and has a
substantial tourism industry. British Columbia has an office in London.

The north

A sparsely populated region. Native peoples (Indians, Inuit) make up a large proportion of the population. Interestingly, the Yukon — once famous for the Gold Rush — boasts the highest proportion of post-secondary certificates, diplomas and degrees in the whole country (39 per cent). It is clearly Canada's intellectual powerhouse!

North West Territories
Population: 58,000; *area:* 1,322,900 sq. miles/3,426,320 sq. km; *main centre:* Yellowknife (12,000)
Department of Education, PO Box 1320, Yellowknife, NT, X1A 2C9.

Yukon Territory
Population: 28,000; *area:* 186,660 sq. miles/ 483,450 sq. km; *main centre:* Whitehorse (16,000)
Department of Education, PO Box 2703, Whitehorse, YT, Y1A 2C6.

LIVING IN CANADA

Although Canada shares a continent with the United States, its citizens are quick to dispel the notion that it is a USA Mk II. 'To an outsider there seems to be very little difference between Canada and the USA,' notes DW. 'However, we see Canada as a compromise between the UK and the USA, and we defend our culture vehemently against American influence.'

Goods tend to cost more in Canada than in the United States. Part of the reason is that items are subject to the Federal Goods and Services Tax and a Provincial Sales Tax. Canadians living close to the border find it more advantageous to cross it to do their shopping in the US. In smaller, more isolated communities the cost of living tends to be quite high and the choice somewhat restricted.

Whether new immigrants avail themselves of the services of Employment and Immigration in Canada or not, most settle down easily in Canada, according to BK. She believes the country offers greater opportunities and a higher standard of living. If there are any drawbacks they are that the country is over-governed and over-taxed.

However, she has never found the climate to be a problem, probably because Canadian houses are well insulated and have efficient central heating systems. 'Despite Canada's subzero temperatures I am warmer in Canada in the winter than in the UK in the summer,' she comments. During the summer temperatures reach the 80s or even the 90s Fahrenheit.

As for the people, MM regards Canadians as 'generous, comfortable, solid, hardworking, quiet, outdoors people. It is a safe place — I can't remember locking my car since I have been here, and only in the last years have we locked the house.' Canadians are also prepared to work hard in order to get ahead.

He has nothing but praise for the amenities. 'It is a great place for bringing up children, and I think the standard of education and the extra-curricular activities offered here are superior to what is available in the UK. The social services here are excellent and the medical coverage via the separate provincial schemes is better than the UK system.'

IMMIGRATION PROSPECTS

Canada has an active immigration programme and accepts more immigrants in relation to its population than any other country. With a falling birthrate the country needs immigrants in order to maintain current population levels. Over a million UK nationals have emigrated there since the war and found it and easy country to settle down in.

A new Immigration Act was implemented on 1st February 1993 which is designed to streamline immigration procedures. The immigration target for 1993 was 250,000 migrants.

Immigration Canada is quite open about the kind of immigrant they are looking for:

- people with good education and training in a variety of fields who have improved their job prospects by updating their skills

- people who have visited Canada in search of employment and demonstrated the demand for their skills by obtaining informal job offers

- people who plan to migrate to an area other than Toronto or Vancouver (though no additional points are offered to such people)

- people who have funds to tide themselves over until a job is found or who have relatives or friends willing to help them settle down.

The current policy envisages placing people in one of three streams:

Stream 1
Applications processed on demand and there is no fixed total:

- immediate family members of people already living in Canada
- people found to be Convention refugees
- people applying through the immigrant investor programme.

● Education	16 maximum
● Age	10 maximum (1)
● Occupational training	18 maximum
● Occupational demand	10 (2)
● Occupational experience	8 maximum (3)
● Arranged employment or designated occupation	10 maximum (3) (4)
● Demographic factor	8 (5)
● Knowledge of English/French	15 maximum (6)
● Personal suitability	10 maximum (7)
● Entrepreneur/investor	45
● Relative over 19 and closer than a cousin	5

1. People aged 21–44 score maximum. Age 45: 8 points; 46: 6 points; 47: 4 points; 48: 2 points.

2. Certain occupations are regarded as priority occupations and attract a higher number of points, but the list is always changing. You can find out the latest state of play by enquiring at the High Commission or perusing the latest edition of *Canada News*.

3. Not available for business migrants.

4. There is a designated occupation list of occupations in greatest demand in individual provinces.

5. A factor used for regulating the number of applicants who meet the selection requirements.

6. 9 points for one language; 15 points for both.

7. Assessment by an immigration officer of your chances of settling down successfully in Canada.

Fig. 14. Points system for emigration to Canada.

Stream 2

Applicants processed on a first-come, first-served basis, with the number in each category subject to limits set in the annual immigration plan:

- parents and grandparents of Canadian resident
- government-assisted and privately sponsored refugees
- applicants who have arranged employment, are self-employed or apply to Canada as live-in care-givers.

Stream 3

Applicants subject to the limits set out in the annual plan and selected on the basis of excellence (i.e. most highly skilled or whose skills are in more demand):

- independent immigrants
- people qualified in designated occupations
- entrepreneurs with business experience.

THE IMMIGRATION PROCESS

In order to determine eligibility for a visa the Canadian Immigration Department assesses people according to a points system based on the criteria given in Figure 14. The pass mark is 70.

Each province has the right to select its own immigrants according to criteria agreed with the Federal Government in Ottawa, but most delegate this responsibility to Ottawa. The exception is Quebec which issues its own selection certificates.

Quebec Province also has different immigration procedures from the rest of Canada. It is not necessary to have an occupation that falls within the Canada Occupations List, provided you have an offer of full-time employment which is validated or attested by the authorities. Also under the family sponsored employment scheme you can be employed by a member of your family who has a business in Quebec. Independent immigrants without jobs are admitted provided they have occupations for which there is a demand. Knowledge of French is another plus.

If you are not sure whether you qualify for an immigrant visa, the Canadian High Commission can provide a free informal assessment (see Fig. 15). If you have a firm offer of employment which has been approved by a Canada employment centre or feel sure that your skills and work experience match immigration requirements, you should make a formal application right away.

IMMIGRATION QUESTIONNAIRE

It is essential that you enclose a stamped self-addressed envelope (at least 6"x9") when returning the attached questionnaire to enable us to respond to your enquiry

TO BE COMPLETED IN BLOCK LETTERS   DATE:

1.
NAME _____
         FAMILY NAME   FIRST NAME

ADDRESS _____

_____

_____

DATE OF BIRTH   D: M: Y: AGE:

2.
SINGLE (NEVER MARRIED) ☐   MARRIED ☐

SEPARATED ☐   ENGAGED ☐

DIVORCED ☐   WIDOWED ☐

NUMBER OF CHILDREN

UNDER 19 YEARS OLD _____

OVER 19 YEARS OLD _____

3. What is your intended occupation in Canada?

4. How many years of experience (after completion of training/apprenticeship) do you have in your intended occupation?

5. What is your present occupation?

6. How long have you been working in your present occupation?

7. Give a brief description of job duties in your present and intended occupation:

Fig. 15. Informal assessment form for emigration to Canada.

120

8. Years of elementary and secondary education _____ Years of apprenticeship/trades training _____

Please list your trade certificate(s)/diplomas: _____

_____

Type of University degree held _____

9. Do you speak: English: Well ☐ With difficulty ☐ Not at all ☐

    French: Well ☐ With difficulty ☐ Not at all ☐

10. If you have a written job offer in Canada, attach a copy.

11. If you, your spouse or any unmarried child has ever been convicted of a crime or offence, attach complete details on a separate sheet.

12. Please outline the value of your assets: Cash: _____

    Property: Current Value: _____ Current Mortgage: _____

    Other (specify) _____

13. Are you planning to open a business or be an investor in Canada?
    If so, describe your proposed business on a separate sheet.

14. Name and address of closest relative in Canada: _____

    _____ Specify Relationship _____

15. What is your destination in Canada? (Name of City and/or Province) _____

16. Spouse's present occupation _____

    Qualifications/diplomas held _____

FOR OFFICIAL USE ONLY

CCDO:	D:	SVP:	T:	Date

A1(a)(11/92)

Fig. 15. Continued.

121

BUSINESS MIGRATION

If you are a potential business migrant there is a special scheme which applies to all provinces with the exception of Quebec. The following questions will help you decide which category you fall into.

- Have you owned, operated or controlled a successful business enterprise?

- Do you have the ability to establish, purchase or make a substantial investment in a new or existing business in Canada? (The amount of investment required varies from province to province. Generally speaking the smaller provinces would require less than Ontario or British Columbia.)

- Will your investment result in the business's creating or continuing employment for at least one Canadian citizen or permanent resident other than you or your family?

- Do you have the ability and experience to provide actual and ongoing participation in the management of the company.

If the answer is yes, you would qualify for the *entrepreneur* category (Stream 3).

- Do you have a net worth of at least C$500,000? For certain provinces it is only necessary to actually transfer C$250,000.

- Are you prepared to invest at least C$250,000 for a minimum of five years in a government accepted investment syndicate or business venture? (Some schemes offer low returns, so beware!).

- Do you have a track record as a successful business person?

If the answer is yes, you would qualify as an *investor* immigrant (Stream 1).

- Have you been successfully employed in a profession or trade?

- Would your qualifications in that occupation be recognised in Canada?

- Do have sufficient money to establish yourself and your family?

If the answer is yes, you would qualify as a *self-employed* immigrant. The type of people who might fall into this category are farmers, artists, writers (Stream 2).

TEMPORARY VISAS

If you have a job offer and only wish to work for a limited time in Canada you need an *employment authorisation* issued by an immigration officer. The normal procedure is as follows:

1. Your employer must give details of your job offer to a Canada Employment Centre (CEC) for approval.

2. The CEC checks whether the employment offer conforms to prevailing pay and working conditions for the occupation concerned and whether the job can be filled by a suitably qualified and available Canadian.

3. The nearest Canadian High Commission visa office contacts you and may invite you for an interview or ask you to send certain documentation.

4. If satisfied, the immigration officer will provide you with the employment authorisation stating that you can work for a *specific period* for a *specific employer*. You must produce this authorisation for the immigration officer at the port of entry into Canada.

If the duties of the job change or the job is extended you should contact the nearest Canada immigration centre before the expiry date of your authorisation.

EDUCATION

State education has a good reputation and is in the hands of the provincial governments. Their offices in London and elsewhere should be able to provide details of the school boards in the place where you intend to reside, otherwise you should contact the Department of Education in the state concerned.

Nationwide:	C$155,000
British Columbia (Vancouver):	C$260,000
Alberta (Edmonton):	C$113,000
Alberta (Calgary):	C$131,000
Saskatchewan (Regina):	C$72,000
Saskatchewan (Saskatoon):	C$75,000
Manitoba (Winnipeg):	C$84,000
Ontario (Toronto):	C$220,000
Ontario (Hamilton):	C$155,000
Ontario (Ottawa):	C$144,000
Quebec (Montreal):	C$115,000
Nova Scotia (Halifax):	C$108,000

To get a rough idea of the annual rent of a two-bedroomed apartment divide by 20.

Fig. 16. Average house prices in Canada, 1993, going from west to east.

One of the features of the Canadian education system is its emphasis on multi-cultural development. Children whose mother tongue is neither English nor French have the opportunity to attend classes in their own language. If you plant to settle in Quebec Province your children will normally be expected to attend schools where the main language of instruction is French.

Higher education is supported by the government, and students' fees only cover 10 per cent of costs. Scholarships, bursaries and government-backed students loans are available.

SOCIAL SECURITY

Medical services are paid for by taxes and are provided by the provincial governments. There is a limited social security agreement between the UK and Canada, but UK contributions do not count towards Canadian benefits.

You should register with the Department of Health of the province in which you reside soon after arrival, and you will be issued with a health card which is valid for that particular province. If you move to another province you must re-apply. Note that certain services (e.g. dentistry and prescriptions) are not covered.

One of the first things you will need to do on arrival is apply for a Social Insurance Number (SIN). Application forms are available from any Canada Employment Centre and post offices.

To qualify for a full Canadian pension you must reside in Canada for 40 years after the age of 18. A minimum period of 10 years' residence will entitle you to one-fortieth of the full rate for each year of residence. You should apply to the nearest Income Security Program office of Health and Welfare Canada.

HOUSE PURCHASE

New immigrants usually prefer to rent accommodation on arrival, though most aim eventually to purchase a house with the help of a mortgage from a bank of trust company. Most houses are detached and have built-in furniture, central heating and air-conditioning — since the summers can be quite hot.

House purchase procedures are fairly similar to those in the UK, with the exception of Quebec Province where it is customary to use a notary. There is considerable variation in house prices as Fig. 16 indicates. The latest edition of Royal Lepage's *Survey of Canadian House Prices* contains up-to-date information on the housing market province by province.

JOB-FINDING

As in most parts of the developed world the service sector is growing fast. The main manufacturing base is in southern Ontario, but there is also some manufacturing industry in Montreal and Vancouver. As in the United States there are stiff laws prohibiting discrimination in the workforce on the grounds of sex, race, creed or age.

Government-backed Canadian Employment Centres throughout the country provide information on jobs and can assist with job-finding, and there are numerous private recruitment consultancies and employment agencies.

When going to a job interview it is advisable to take the following documentation:

- passport, birth certificate;
- certificates of your qualifications
- testimonials
- record of landing (visa)
- social insurance number
- provincial health insurance number
- driving licence.

One matter which newcomers may find confusing is that while your qualifications may be accepted in one province, if you move to another you may have to requalify.

MIGRATION CONSULTANTS IN THE UK

Hall Carriere, BCL Immigration Services. Several Canada-based immigration consultancies and lawyers advertise in *Canada News*.

FURTHER INFORMATION

Employment and Immigration Canada produce some useful immigration fact sheets on Employment, Housing, Education, Health and Social Security, and so on, as well as more substantial booklets (e.g. *Living in Canada, A Newcomer's Guide to Canada*) and these are available from most High Commission offices.

The provincial governments of Alberta, British Columbia, Quebec and Saskatchewan have offices in London and can provide information and addresses for their respective provinces.

BCL Immigration Services organises seminars on Canada and the USA.

Canada News (Outbound Newspapers) is the only regular newspaper published in the UK which has up-to-date information on Canada and its immigration procedures. The Bibliography lists some useful books.

Notes
[1] *A Book of Canada*, William Toye (1962).

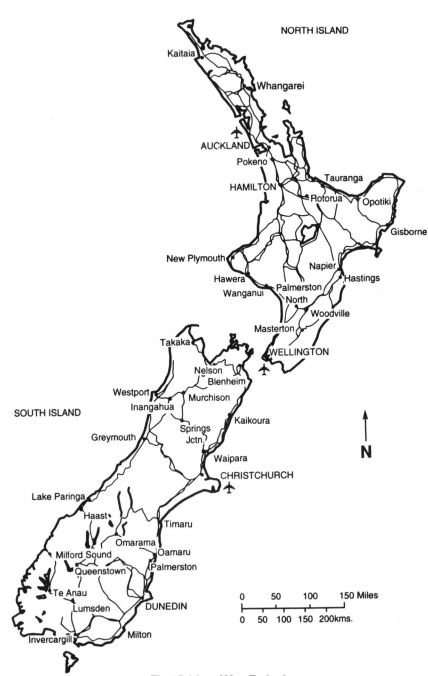

Fig. 17. Map of New Zealand.

128

10
New Zealand

If an English butler and an English nanny sat down to design a country they would come up with New Zealand. (Anon)

The great drawback of New Zealand comes from the feeling that after crossing the world and journeying over so many miles you have not at all succeeded in getting away from England. (Anthony Trollope)[1]

Of all the countries surveyed in this book New Zealand is perceived as the one that is most similar to the UK. It is of a similar size (103,735 sq. miles) and relatively compact: only 800 miles separate Auckland in the north from Invercargill the most southerly town in New Zealand. (Lands End to John O'Groats is just under 600 miles.) The climate, too is similar, though the terrain is more mountainous with 75 per cent of the country above 600 feet.

The great difference is the population size. Currently around 3.5 million people live in New Zealand, which means that the country is quite sparsely populated. This is especially true of the South Island where there is plenty of grand scenery and undisturbed wilderness.

Some newly arrived immigrants experience a sense of isolation, for New Zealand is a long way from anywhere else. Australia, for instance, is some 1,000 miles away and Europe is on the other side of the world. Air travel, of course, has made the world seem much smaller, but, even so, to travel out of New Zealand is an expensive business.

New Zealand boasts that it is a multi-racial society — a tradition that dates back to the Treaty of Waitangi in 1840 between the British authorities and Maori chiefs. Nearly one-fifth are of non-European origin. In addition to the Maoris, there are Chinese (the first of whom arrived with the gold rushes of the nineteenth century), Indians originally from the sugar cane fields of Fiji, and in this century migrants from all over Polynesia. More recently there has been an influx from Hong Kong and South East Asia. The majority of the population, however, is of British or Irish descent, so immigrants from the British Isles should have few difficulties in settling down.

'New Zealand society contains a deep humanitarian streak, one which is reflected in the egalitarian social policies erected to protect residents from the vicissitudes of a laissez-faire economic system,' writes R.J. Johnston[2]. With its centralised bureaucratic structure the country has been more successful than most in eliminating poverty and deprivation.

THE ECONOMY

In the mid-1980s New Zealand's economy was in the doldrums, but the Government has brought in a number of reforms which have rejuvenated it. Above all it has committed itself to providing a stable, investor-friendly, deregulated environment for business growth.

The policy seems to be working, for in 1992 New Zealand won recognition as the OECD country best adapted for long-term competitiveness. The economy has also received a welcome boost with the establishment of CER (the Australia New Zealand Closer Economic Relation Trade Agreement) which in effect increases the domestic market base to about 19 million people.

Although there are far more sheep in the country than people — 60 million to be precise — that does not mean that the economy is overwhelmingly agricultural. Less than half the country's export earnings are now derived from dairy products, meat and wool, compared with 84 per cent in 1966.

The country has a growing manufacturing base, which now accounts for more than a quarter of New Zealand's exports — a tenfold increase in less than thirty years. Major export earners include processed foods, wood products, industrial chemicals, household goods and scientific equipment. The software industry is going from strength to strength and the wine industry has gained international recognition. The tourism industry is very buoyant and the educational institutions attract large numbers of foreign students.

NORTH ISLAND

Around three-quarters of the population live on North Island which contains Auckland, the country's largest and most cosmopolitan city with a population approaching the million mark. Wellington (pop. 400,000) in the south of the island is capital of New Zealand and it is here that the government and many company head offices are situated. Other areas of note are Waikato (a major dairy region), Tarnaki with its oil and gas industry, Gisborne (a major fruit and wine-growing area), and the Bay of Plenty (where the famous thermal springs of Rotorua are situated).

SOUTH ISLAND

Christchurch, situated on the fertile Canterbury Plans, is the largest city on the South Island and regarded as the most 'English' part of New Zealand. It was originally established as a model settlement by the Anglican Church. The Scottish Presbyterians had a similar plan to Dunedin (pop. 107,000) which consequently boasts many buildings which bear a striking resemblance to those in Scotland. Across the Cook Strait from Wellington is Nelson/Marlborough, a major wine and food producing centre. The West Coast and Southland (in the south-west) are noted for their spectacular and rugged scenery.

IMMIGRATION PROSPECTS

Since 1840 750,000 migrants have arrived in New Zealand. However the days of unrestricted immigration are at an end, and today only 16 per cent of current New Zealand residents were born overseas. The Government now takes a cautious line on immigration, preferring to take in only as many immigrants as it feels can be absorbed into the economy.

This means tight immigration controls. Although the current target figure of 25,000 approvals per year may sound reasonable, you should bear in mind that it does not refer to the British Isles alone, but it is a world-wide quota. The country accepts immigrants from all over the world these days — not just the British Isles.

The 1991 Immigration Act brought in a number of changes. It is no longer necessary for an applicant to have a job offer or an occupation on Approved Occupation List. More emphasis is placed on establishing that the skills and strengths of each applicant will prove an asset to New Zealand.

If you have close relations in New Zealand, you enjoy an advantage over other applicants, since you will receive precedence over other categories of immigrant. Some 45 per cent of immigrants fall into the Family Category, though the proportion is often exceeded. (In February 1993, for instance, they accounted for 58 per cent of permanent resident approvals.)

The remaining places are offered to people hoping to qualify for immigrant status on the strength of their skills, qualifications or business expertise. People who reach the automatic pass mark (currently 28) should, however, have few problems in gaining approval.

If you do not reach the automatic pass mark, your application will be placed in the 'pool'. Here the future is less certain, since in recent times there have been far more applicants than places available. The numbers of approvals are regulated by raising or lowering the pass mark for the pool. (In 1993 only applicants with scores of 26 or 27 were recommended for approval.)

People with no qualifications claiming work experience points will need to be in an occupation mentioned on the Government's Approved Occupation List. However, with the 'pool' pass mark set so high, it is unlikely that a person in this category would gain sufficient points to gain approval under the General category.

Even if you have passed the self-assessment exercise with flying colours, you should not regard approval as automatic. There are other hurdles to be surmounted: New Zealand health requirements are very strict; the immigration service may regard certain qualifications as inappropriate or not recognise them; they also take a dim view of anyone with a criminal record — however slight.

Your application could also be rejected on technical grounds, such as insufficient documentation (e.g. qualification certificates, evidence of work experience), and your rights to appeal are restricted if you make a mistake with your application. For this reason an increasing number of migrants are using the services of migration consultants that can make a good case for their clients and ensure that nothing is missed out in the application.

It is worth noting that immigration policy never remains static, and modifications are brought in from time to time to ensure that immigration continues to meet the economic needs of the country.

IMMIGRATION CHECKLIST

To determine whether you are likely to be accepted for immigration to New Zealand, work your way through the following questionnaire.

1.   Have you a close relative living permanently in New Zealand who is willing to sponsor you?

     YES   Go to 2.
     NO   Go to 3 — or 5 if you are a business investor.

2.   Does your relationship fall into one of the following categories?

- a parent all of whose children live outside your home country
- a parent with at least half your children living in New Zealand
- an unmarried dependent child under 17 (20 in some cases)
- a spouse/partner.

    YES   Provided you can provide evidence of your family relationship and the residence status of your family members you qualify for residence under the Family category.
    NO   Go to 3.

3. Provided you are under 55 you may well qualify for residence on the basis of your qualifications, work experience, age and settlement factors. Assess yourself according to the points system. Do you score 28 or more? [a]

    YES   You qualify automatically for residence under the General Category.
    NO   Go to 4.

4. Have you scored between 20 and 27? [b]

    YES   You will go into a global pool from which monthly draws are taken. Alternatively, if you have business expertise, go to 5.
    NO   Go to 5.

5. Perhaps you have owned and operated a business. If so, do you score a minimum of 7 points for qualifications and/or work experience on the points system?

    YES   Go to 6.
    NO   It does not look as if you meet the residence criteria.

6. Have you sufficient business and investment funds [c] and can you show they are the direct result of your own business or skills over a period of at least three years? If so, you qualify under the Business Investment category.

Notes

a   Pass mark 1993.
b   In February 1993 only would-be migrants attaining scores of 26 and 27 gained approval.

c   A minimum of $NZ 750,000 in passive investment; a minimum of $NZ
    625,000 in a commercial venture in Auckland or Wellington; a minimum of
    $NZ 500,000 in other areas.

GENERAL CATEGORY — POINTS SYSTEM

In November 1991 New Zealand introduced the points system to assess
the calibre of potential immigrants based on:

● qualifications: ranging from 15 points for a postgraduate degree or
  first degree in science or technology to 2 points for 12 years' schooling

● work experience: points are awarded for every two years of relevant
  work experience in an approved occupation up to a maximum of ten
  points

● age: number of points declines with age after 29; there is an age limit
  of 55

● settlement factors: settlement funds, sponsorship, investment funds,
  an offer of skilled employment.

See fig. 18.

NON-IMMIGRANTS

While it is possible for a British passport holder to visit New Zealand for
up to six months without the need of a visa for business or vacation
purposes, you cannot normally take up employment — except perhaps on
a casual basis, in which case you would need to apply for a work permit
when you are in New Zealand.

Work visas
If you have made arrangements to take up a job you must apply for a work
visa before you leave the UK. Your applications must be supported by an
offer of employment from a New Zealand employer who is able to
demonstrate that he or she cannot find people of equivalent skills locally
to fill the post. Ideally the occupation should be on the Approved Occupation List. The maximum length of a work visa is three years, though it
is renewable.

One-year work visas

Under-30s with no dependent children are eligible to apply for one-year work visas. These are available on a first come first served basis and numbers are currently limited to 500 per year. In 1993 the quota was filled up soon after the opening date for applications on 1st May. Applicants need to have return air tickets and evidence of financial support (currently around £1,500). This is a new scheme which could be modified or withdrawn in future years.

SOCIAL SECURITY

New Zealand has a well-developed welfare state. The social security scheme is non-contributory and financed from general taxation. Hospital treatment is virtually free, but those who can afford to now pay the majority of their doctors' and other health-care fees, and so private health insurance is now growing in important.

There is a social security agreement between the UK and New Zealand (see leaflet SA8 obtainable from the Benefits Agency). If you are emigrating permanently to New Zealand your residence in the UK will count towards satisfying New Zealand residence tests for benefit.

The benefits covered by the agreement are:

● Unemployment — income tested
● National Superannuation (pension)
● Widow's Benefit — income tested
● Orphan's Benefits
● Family Benefit (i.e. child allowance)
● Invalid's Benefit — income tested.

For more information contact the High Commission or the Department of Social Welfare in Wellington.

EDUCATION

Education is of a high standard with 90 per cent of children benefiting from some form of pre-schooling. Education in state schools is free and more than 100 private schools receive a state subsidy. The school year is divided into three terms: February to May; May to August; September to December. Secondary education leads to School Certificate (equivalent to GCSE Grades 1 to 3), Sixth Form Certificate and Higher School Certificate (equivalent to GCE A Level).

General Category - Points System

Self assessment

Note: If you achieve a points score below 20 you are unlikely to meet the requirements for Residence in New Zealand under the General Category.

Principal applicants who are over age 55 or who cannot meet the minimum English language requirement will not be approved.

POINTS FACTOR	POINTS	YOUR SCORE
EMPLOYABILITY FACTORS Points may be scored for both Qualifications and Work Experience		
1. Qualifications:		
Sucessful completion of 12 years schooling	2	
Diploma or Certificate at least 1 year and less than 2 years full time study	4	
Diploma or Certificate from 2 years to 3 years full time study	8	
Bachelor's degree in any area of study not mentioned below or a Trade Certificate or Advanced Trade Qualification	12	
Post graduate degree or a Bachelor's degree in any science, technical or engineering area of study	15	
2.Work Experience: (Must be relevant to Post Secondary Qualifications or in an Approved Occupation)		
2 years	1	
4 years	2	
6 years	3	
8 years	4	
10 years	5	
12 years	6	
14 years	7	
16 years	8	
18 years	9	
20 years	10	
Maximum points for Employability factor: 25		

Fig. 18. Self-assessment form for emigration to New Zealand.

POINTS FACTOR	POINTS	YOUR SCORE
3. Age		
18 -24 years	8	
25 -29 years	10	
30 -34 years	8	
35 -39 years	6	
40 -44 years	4	
45 -49 years	2	
Maximum age limit: 55 years		
Maximum points for Age factor: 10		
4. Settlement Factors		
N7 $ 100.000 settlement funds	2	
Family sponsor **OR**	2	
Community Sponsor	3	
1 point for each additional NZ $100,000 investment funds,		
up to a max of $300,000	3	
Offer of Skilled employment	3	
Maximum points for Settlement factors: 5		
MAXIMUM POINTS: 40 **TOTAL:**		

There is a substantial number of private schools listed in a directory published by the Independent Schools Council. At the higher level New Zealand boasts 25 technical institutes, community colleges and independent business college plus seven universities of good repute.

JOB-FINDING

The Employment and Vocational Guidance Service of the Department of Labour provides a comprehensive job placement service and has branches at 50 locations throughout the country. The Careers Information Section publishes leaflets on educational opportunities and careers.

The Public Service Official Circular advertises details of all public service jobs, while the *Education Gazette* publishes details of all teaching jobs. Private recruitment consultants are listed under Employment Agencies in *Yellow Pages*. The Wednesday and Saturday editions of the newspapers carry job vacancies.

There are a number of private recruitment consultants and agencies, the leading one being the Sheffield Group, which has representation in the UK. Organisations such as Ranfurly Johnston Mackey, Job Search and LEADS can also provide assistance.

HOUSING AND CARS

The average price of a house in 1993 was $NZ127,000, but there is considerable variation from place to place. Auckland is the most expensive city. The estate agents Harcourt publish the Blue Book series of real estate magazines for different regions of the country which are available from Consyl Publishing. Two other national estate agents are listed in the directory. House purchase follows UK practice.

It is worth while to investigate the merits of purchasing a car on arrival and shipping one. There could be various tax savings if you choose the latter course. Indeed, at present if you take a car which you have owned for a year with you to New Zealand, it can enter the country free of customs duty and other taxes. If you sell it within two years duty and taxes must be paid.

MIGRATION CONSULTANTS

Ranfurly Johnston Mackey, Malcolm Consultants, Sperry & Associates, Network Migration Ltd.

FURTHER INFORMATION

The Immigration Department at New Zealand House has a number of booklets and leaflets on life in New Zealand including *About New Zealand, Education in New Zealand* and *New Zealand in Outline*. The New Zealand Trade Development Board published a comprehensive *Investment Pack* available from the Trade Commission. The Information Officer can provide up-to-date information on most non-immigration matters including a list of useful addresses.

New Zealand Outlook, a bi-monthly newspaper for visitors and emigrants to New Zealand, contains up-to-date information on visa requirements and the current economic situation. *New Zealand News UK* is a weekly newspaper which contains coverage of events in New Zealand and includes items of interest to prospective migrants.

Consyl Publishing distribute a number of books about New Zealand including *The New Zealand Education Directory*, the monthly *Business Review* and various real-estate periodicals. Malcolm Consultants distribute *The New Zealand Directory* a glossy brochure which contains useful articles on life in New Zealand including personal accounts.

Notes
[1] Anthony Trollope, *Australia and New Zealand* (1873).
[2] R.J. Johnston, *The New Zealanders: How They Live and Work*, David Charles, 1976.

HOW TO LIVE & WORK IN NEW ZEALAND   Joy Muirhead

A new immigration policy and growing economy have turned New Zealand into one of the most sought after destinations for people seeking a new life overseas. Its clean environment and healthy lifestyles are added attractions for thousands of new migrants today. Written by a British expat who has lived in New Zealand for more than 20 years, this timely and practical book meets a pressing need for information on everything from making the decision to go, coping with the migration process, to settling in to a new home, job or business, and starting out on a new life in this beautiful country. Joy Muirhead settled in New Zealand in 1972. Married to a New Zealander she has raised a family through school and university in New Zealand and worked for a number of New Zealand accountancy, catering, farming and real estate companies.

£9.99, 208pp illus. 1 85703 090 7.

Please add postage & packing (UK £1.00 per copy. Europe £2.00 per copy. World £3.00 per copy airmail). How To Books Ltd, Plymbridge House, Estover Road, Plymouth PL6 7PZ, United Kingdom. Tel: (0752) 695745. Fax: (0752) 695699. Telex: 45635.

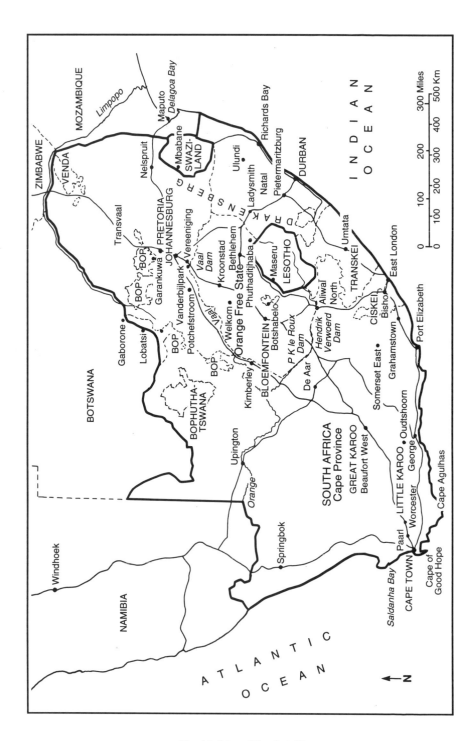

Fig. 19. Map of South Africa

140

11
South Africa

> Since Jan van Riebeeck's time South Africa has attracted settlers from the corners of the globe. Today the country's cultural diversity is one of its most dynamic components. *(South Africa Travel Guide)*

> We shall never be able to have complete peace in South Africa as long as there is statutory discrimination. (F.W. De Kleerk)

Of all the countries mentioned in this book South Africa stands in a class of its own. It is in a sense a microcosm of the world with ethnic diversity and disparities in economic and social development. Although by far the most advanced country in sub-Saharan Africa, it is still in many respects a Third World country where only a minority enjoy living standards on a par with (if not better than) countries in North America and Western Europe.

It is also a nation which is currently undergoing profound political and economic changes, which make it difficult to predict its future direction. Will it become a shining example of a multi-racial society with everyone pulling together to create a sound economy? Or will it degenerate into chaos and civil war like some of its neighbours to the north, its economy in tatters?

THE POLITICAL AND HISTORICAL BACKGROUND

Although this book does not set out to take a political stance, any prospective emigrant needs to have an appreciation of South African politics and history since they will affect him or her in some way. One of the fundamental tenets from the time of Dutch colonial rule (1652–1795) has been racial segregation — apartheid. In effect this meant that the whites were a privileged class while the other races enjoyed few rights and were subject to many restrictions.

During this century the policy intensified. Pass laws came into being prohibiting the free movement of blacks; the Mixed Marriages Act prohibited marriages between people of different races; the Group Areas Act prescribed where and with whom people could live; the best jobs were reserved for the whites. Members of different racial groups were prevented from belonging to the same political party and an attempt was made to segregate blacks into tribal states (homelands) most of which were little more than barren wildernesses.

Millions of blacks were caught up in a cycle of poverty because of the constraints places upon them, and a growing number began to agitate for a better deal. World opinion came to their support, and country after country condemned the apartheid policy and applied sanctions against South Africa. Faced with pressures from inside and outside the republic the South African Government has started to dismantle apartheid.

This step was inevitable, for not only was the system of separate development politically unjust, it did not make economic sense either. All the homelands were dependent on massive handouts from Pretoria, and jobs there were few and far between. To implement apartheid with separate courts, separate schools, separate hospitals, separate leisure amenities, led to tremendous duplication of effort and a bloated civil service. Labour laws meant that industry and commerce were forced to recruit on racial lines rather than on the basis of ability.

In April 1994 South Africa holds its first elections on the basis of one man one vote, and this is likely to mean an end to white rule and a black majority in pariiament for the first time. By the time most people come to read this book, the elections will have taken place and we will be in a better position to judge how the county will shape up in the future.

If extremist political elements gain control or seek to disrupt the process, the future could be fraught with problems. However, South Africa's black political leaders seem to be level-headed people, for the most part, who recognise the need for a stable and successful economy if they are to improve the well-being of their supporters. The last thing they want to do is upset the apple-cart and discourage investment.

It is against this background that you need to consider your emigration plans.

THE COUNTRY

South Africa has a population of around 35 million and covers an area of 471,445 sq. miles (1,221,031 sq. km). It is a federal national of which Pretoria (pop. 825,000) is the administrative capital, Cape Town the legislative capital and Bloemfontein the judicial capital. It is divided into four provinces:

Cape Province

Population: 5.5 million; *area:* 644,060 sq. km; *capital:* Cape Town (2 million); *main cities:* Port Elizabeth (650,000); East London (170,000)
South Africa's largest province is situated in the southern and western part of the country. Much of the industry is centred around Cape Town in the west and Port Elizabeth.

Natal

Population: 2.1 million; *area:* 91,740 sq. km; *capital:* Pietermaritzburg (195,000); *other cities:* Durban (635,000)
This is the eastern part of South Africa. Its main industrial area is based on Durban which is the centre of the country's sugar-growing and processing industry. It is also a popular place for tourism with game parks and seaside resorts.

Orange Free State

Population: 2 million; *area:* 125,930 sq. km; *capital:* Bloemfontein (235,000)
The central part of South Africa on the highveld of the central plateau bordered by the Transvaal, Natal, Lesotho and Cape Province.

Transvaal

Population: 8.6 million; *area:* 265,470 sq. km; *capital:* Johannesburg (1.6 million)
The northern part of South Africa bordering Botswana, Zimbabwe, Mozambique and Swaziland; 54 per cent of the white population live here and the southern Transvaal is the most important industrial centre in the country producing the whole of the country's gold and half of its manufacturing output. Most companies have their headquarters in Johannesburg.

Other territories

In addition there are the self-governing territories of KwaZulu, Gazanzulu, Lebowa, Qwaqwa, KaNgwane, Kwandebele and the Republics of Bophuthatswana, Venda, Ciskei and Transkei.

THE PEOPLE

In most countries of sub-Saharan Africa the population is overwhelmingly African. In South Africa whilst the majority are African there are three substantial ethnic minorities. Let us have a quick look at the main racial groups.

The whites

Most of the 5 million whites are descended from Dutch, French, British and German immigrants who settled in the country between the seventeenth and nineteenth centuries. More recently there has been a substantial influx of Portuguese, many from Angola and Mozambique; 56 per cent are Afrikaans-speaking; 38 per cent are English-speaking.

The vast majority of the whites live in urban areas, over 50 per cent in the Transvaal, especially in the Pretoria/Johannesburg/Vereeniging region which boasts a large and influential Jewish community. The second largest concentration is in the South West Cape region; and the third major area is Durban/Pietermaritzburg. On the whole the lifestyle of the whites is on a par with that of people in the developed world.

The blacks

The 25 million blacks represent the largest segment of the population and 50 per cent live in rural areas. The standard of living of many of them is on a par with other countries of southern Africa, and up till now they have had to be content with inferior health facilities, education and housing. Yet despite these handicaps there is now a burgeoning African middle-class and some Africans have become millionaires.

The Africans are drawn from a number of tribal/linguistic groups: Zulu, North Sotho, Xhosa, South Sotho, Tswana, Shangaan-Tsanga, Swazi, South Ndebele, Venda. While tribalism may still play a role in rural areas, it has vanished in the towns.

The coloureds

There are 3.2 million people of mixed race and over 85 per cent of them live in Cape Province. The main sub-groups are the Griquas of Hottentot-European ancestry and the Cape Malays who were brought to the Cape by the East India Company and follow the Islamic tradition.

The Asians

The majority of the million or so Asians are Indians whose ancestors came to South Africa as indentured labourers to work on the sugar plantations in Natal where the majority of them still live. Many are prosperous merchants, traders and professional people.

IMMIGRATION POLICY

Not long ago the aim of South Africa's immigration policy was to increase the number of white settlers. Indians were encouraged to return to India. But in the post-apartheid era such a stance is no longer acceptable.

The current policy is now more in line with that of other countries in this book: to attract immigrants not on the basis of their colour but on the skills they have to offer. Educated blacks are particularly welcome as the country strives to overcome the racial imbalance in skills.

However, South Africa has a problem common with many Third World countries: chronic unemployment —as high as 45 per cent. It may therefore seem strange that immigration should be encouraged at all. The raison d'être for going ahead is the fact that each skilled immigrant is reckoned to create 4–7 jobs, even if he or she is not making any investment in the country.

There are no hard and fast immigration rules for South Africa — no points system by which you can work out your eligibility. Applications are treated individually and on their own merits. While the country is keen to attract immigrants with skills and capital, it does not set targets, but reacts to the needs of the economy.

Normally you cannot obtain a work permit once you are in South Africa; this has to be done before your leave — a process which takes up to three months from the time of the initial job offer. However, if you are needed urgently the shortened immigration procedure takes a matter of hours.

IMMIGRATION PROCEDURES

First of all decide which category of migrant you fall into.

Worker category

This is for people who have jobs or wish to find employment. South Africa has no list of approved professions, but applicants have to be professionally qualified. Moreover the employer has to demonstrate to the Department of Manpower that the skills you offer cannot be found locally. (Settlers may not change their occupation as recorded on their permits for permanent residence unless approval has been obtained from the Department of Home Affairs but this rule could change.)

Financial independent person

This would suit a self-employed person who has a minimum of £100,000 to invest in South Africa. If you are considering retiring to South Africa the amount of pension you are receiving would also be considered.

There is one further category, the Family Reunion Scheme, whereby you

PRELIMINARY IMMIGRATION QUESTIONNAIRE

Full Names (Dr/Mr/Mrs/Miss) ....
Address ....
.... Tel No. ....
Age .... Date of Birth ....
Married/Never Married/Divorced/Separated: to be divorced on (date) ....
Widowed/To be Married: Before/After Emigration
Your nationality .... Your country of birth ....
Your wife's nationality .... Your wife's country of birth ....
Do you or any of your dependants suffer or have any of you ever suffered from any physical or mental disability?
(Yes of No) .... If yes, give full details ....
....
Number of children who will accompany you: .... State ages: ....
Details regarding children over the age of 15 years:-

Name	Age	Qualifications	Occupation	For Offical Use
....	....	....	....	
....	....	....	....	

Have you or your wife ever resided in or visited South Africa? ....
If so, please give details and period (dates) of visit/residence: ....
....
Have you or your wife ever applied/registered for permanent residence? (Yes or no) .... If so
Quote Permit no. ....

(A) SCHOOL EDUCATION
Total number of years schooling: ....
Primary School .... From: .... To: ....
Secondary/High School .... From: .... To: ....
Professional School .... From: .... To: ....
Certificates obtained ....
Specify Subjects and Grade ....
....

(B) HIGHER EDUCATION OR SPECIAL TRAINING
Name of University, College or Institution attended: ....
Prescribed duration of course ....
Period attended .... From .... To ....
Major subjects ....
....
Degree diploma or certificate obtained ....
....

(C) TRADE QUALIFICATIONS
Duration of apprenticeship training .... From: .... To: ....
Trade in which qualified ....
year in which qualified ....
To which trade union do you belong? ....
To which section of the union ....
(Skilled, semi-skilled, unskilled) ....

(D) LANGUAGE PROFICIENCY
(a) What is your mother language? ....
(b) What is your proficiency in other language? (Answer YES or NO under the different headings)

	SPEAK	READ	WRITE
(i) English	....	....	....
(ii) Afrikaans	....	....	....
(iii)	....	....	....
(iv)	....	....	....

Fig. 20. Preliminary immigration questionnaire for South Africa.

(E) RECORD OF EMPLOYMENT

The details furnished below must be in date order (including periods of unemployment) for the last 20 years.

For Offical Use	Name of Firm	City/Town in which located	From	To	Nature of your work

(F) Describe your present/last duties: ....

....

(G) What is the trade or business of your present/last employer? ....

....

(H) What is your present/last Salary or Wage? .... per Week/Month/Annum
(Please specify)

(I) What specific occupation do you intend following in South Africa? ....

....

....

(J) What amount of money will you transfer/take to South Africa? ....

(K) Do you receive a pension or private income, please give details and state ....
amcunts. ....

(L) Have you an offer of employment in South Africa? ....(If so, the
original letter of appointment must be attached. If negotiations are still in
progress, please await the final outcome before submitting this form).

(M) Details regarding relatives and/or friends resident in South Africa.

Name	Address	Relationship/Acquaintanceship

(N) General remarks ....

....

....

Signature of Applicant   Date

On completion, please return to the Chief Migration Officer, Immigration Section, South African Embassy, Trafalgar Square, London WC2N 5DP.

REMARKS BY CHIEF MIGRATION OFFICER

....
....
....

....

DATE   CHIEF MIGRATION OFFICER

BI 897 (IM88)

can be sponsored by close relatives. Because of the recession sponsorship has fallen largely into abeyance, but that does not mean it will not be revived as and when the economy improves.

Immigration officials set four basic criteria for issuing a visa:

● Can you contribute positively to South Africa?
● Are you depriving a South African citizen of employment?
● Will your standard of living be jeopardised if you move to South Africa?
● Have you any experience of living in South Africa?

It is usual for an emigrant to be sent a preliminary questionnaire for completion. If the authorities consider you are eligible for permanent residence you will be required to forward documentation to support your application. In some cases a copy authenticated by a solicitor will suffice, but you should check with the immigration office first. The following documentation is normally required:

● full birth certificate

● photographs (of yourself and accompanying dependants)

● medical certificate

● X ray certificate

● abridged CV

● marriage certificate

● character reference (may be waived)

● qualification certificates

● policy certificates from all countries you have resided in since the age of 18; (this does not apply to residence in the UK)

● work references for the past 5 years (or affidavit in certain circumstances).

You may also have to supply the following:

● the original deed poll, if you have changed your name

● (in the case of divorcees) the divorce certificate and (for the man) a form signed by your ex-wife stating that you have informed her of your plans to leave the country and that you have made arrangements for maintenance, and so on.

CITIZENSHIP

It is not necessary to take out South African citizenship in order to secure permanent residence in South Africa. However, at present any children of yours aged between 15 and 25 will automatically become South African citizens if they reside in the country for more than five years. There is no longer any liability for them to perform military service.

FINANCIAL CONSIDERATIONS

Like many countries in Africa, South Africa has strict exchange control regulations, designed to attract investment and ensure that funds stay inside the country. Residents are not free to repatriate funds as and when they wish; in fact you will only be able to do so if you leave South Africa for good.

While certain payments (e.g. maintenance orders) are exempt, others (e.g. school fees, insurance premiums) may cause problems. For this reason and the fact that the rand is likely to decline in value, there is much to be said for keeping some financial assets outside South Africa. It would also be sensible to take out a life insurance policy in the UK or offshore in case your survivors wish to return to the UK or move elsewhere on your decease.

On the other hand the system can work in favour of migrants. At the time of writing there are two exchange rates for the South African rand. The normal rate is known as the Commercial Rand and used for trade transactions and by visitors to South Africa. The Financial Rand is for approved investment in South Africa and offers you a better exchange rate (i.e. more rand for your pound or other approved foreign currency).

As a concession, immigrants to South Africa are normally allowed to bring in capital at the Financial Rand rate chiefly for the purchase of a house and car. (There is a limit of R500,000.) In effect, this means that you can buy a house at a considerable discount — perhaps as much as 50 per cent. However, these arrangements could well change in the future, and you should make sure you obtain the latest information.

A number of restrictions are placed on permanent residents of which you need to be aware. For instance, you may not use overseas credit cards when in South Africa. There are a number of South African banks in London which can advise on these and other matters, and you should seek the advice of one of them at an early stage.

COST OF LIVING

The rand is not a particularly strong currency: the exchange rate is affected by the gold price and is liable to fluctuate. In order to compare prices it is best not to convert from sterling using the official exchange rate, since this underestimate the purchasing power of the rand.

One suggestion is to multiply a sterling amount by 2.5 or 3 in order to get the equivalent value in rand. Thus a £20,000 salary would be equivalent to between R50,000 and R60,000.

However certain items (car, electrical consumer goods) are expensive and you should consider importing these as personal effects, on which you will not normally have to pay duty. A booklet entitled *Living Costs in South Africa* is obtainable from the South African Embassy.

HOUSING

Normally people start off in temporary accommodation in a hotel or boarding house which are relatively inexpensive. Rented housing is available in some areas, and employers often provide subsidised rented accommodation to their employees.

If you are taking up permanent residence you will doubtless want to purchase a house of your own — more often than not a bungalow. Detached houses stand in their own grounds; so-called town houses are often detached but they are within a compound where there are communal gardens.

Prices are lower than in the UK, especially if you are buying outright with the Financial Rand (see Fig. 21). Mortgages (known as bonds) are available from building societies of up to 80 per cent of the value of the property. You may, however, find that your employer will assist with house purchase.

Estate agents are qualified in the initial legalities of house purchase and will normally escort you to properties. Their commission — payable by the purchaser — is around 6 per cent plus VAT. It is common for both seller and purchaser to use the same lawyer (as in France) who is normally appointed by the seller, though the buyer pays the fees.

When you have chosen a house you sign a legally binding contract and decide on a completion date. In order to protect yourself from contingencies it is advisable to insert certain suspensive clauses in the contract, but the more of these there are the less attractive your offer becomes.

To discourage property speculation you are currently required to lodge the deeds of your property with the bank for five years.

	Houses with communal gardens	*Detached*
Johannesburg:	R 200,000–R350,000	R 400,000 upwards
Durban:	R 120,000–R 300,000	R 300,000 upwards
Garden Route	R 300,000 upwards	R 300,000 upwards
Cape Peninsula	R 110,000 upwards	R 200,000 upwards

Fig. 21. Sample house prices, 1993, South Africa.

One or two South African estate agents have offices in London and can give you a more precise idea of house prices from place to place.

HEALTH AND SOCIAL SECURITY

There is no equivalent to the National Health Service in South Africa. However, it is common for companies to subscribe to private medical schemes on behalf of their employees.

EDUCATION

Education is in the hands of the provincial governments and school hours are usually from 8 am to 1.30 pm. The medium of instruction is either English or Afrikaans.

There are around 200 private schools in South Africa, many of them with strong Church connections. The majority now receive grants from provincial governments. Lists of the schools are available from the Independent Schools Council, the Catholic Institute of Education, and the SA Board of Jewish Education.

There is a developed further education sector and there are English medium universities in Cape Town, Durban, Grahamstown (Rhodes), Pietermaritzburg, Johannesburg (Witwatersrand).

MIGRATION CONSULTANTS

Mallinick, Ress, Richman & Closenberg.

JOBSEARCH

The Kent based SA Placements (part of the St Thomas Group) has contact with agents and employers throughout South Africa and is able to process applications. Would-be immigrants are offered an insight into the South African jobs market at their regular one-day seminars. If you are planning to make a trip to South Africa they can arrange meetings with potential employers.

SETTLING IN

If you need help in settling down in South Africa, you should consider contacting the 1820 Settlers Association of South Africa. This charitable association was established in 1920 to encourage migration to South Africa and works closely with the Department of Homes Affairs, industry and commerce. It offers the following free benefits to members:

● assistance in settling in South Africa (including housing/accommodation, finance, legal and medical matters, education)

● subsidised travel abroad

● bursaries for tertiary education

● help with obtaining residence permits, work permits, study permits, driving licences or any of the statutory requirements from the Department of Home Affairs

● social and cultural functions

● subscription to *The Settler* and regional newsletters

● employment opportunities

● welfare and pensions assistance

● help in obtaining South African citizenship.

There are branches in East London, Post Elizabeth, Vereenigung, Durban and Cape Town. The UK representative is Outbound Newspapers.

FURTHER INFORMATION

The South African Embassy can provide a number of useful leaflets including *Living in South Africa, Living Costs in South Africa, Employment in South Africa, Educational Facilities in South Africa*; and also more substantial publications: *Mini Atlas of Southern Africa*

The South African Tourism Board's *Travel Guide* (quoted at the beginning of this chapter) contains useful maps of all the regions of the country.

Bear in mind that South Africa is in a state of flux and the information in this chapter can quickly go out of date.

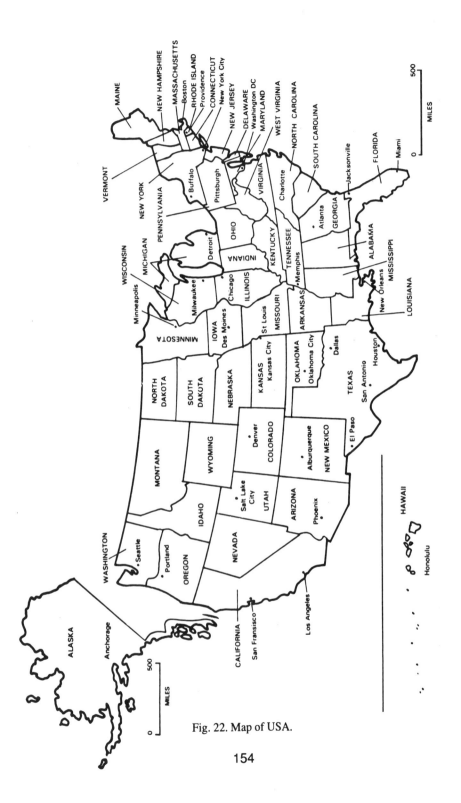

Fig. 22. Map of USA.

154

12
United States of America

The United States is the greatest single achievement of European civilisation. (R.B. Mowat, *The United States of America*) [1]

America is a large friendly dog in a small room. Every time it wags its tail it knocks over a chair. (A.J. Toynbee) [2]

Ever since 1584 when Sir Walter Raleigh first set foot on Bodie Island in what is now North Carolina and claimed the 600 sq. miles of territory on behalf of the English Crown the United States has been a magnet for migrants from all over the world.

In the early years of the seventeenth century America attracted settlers from Sweden, Holland, France and Germany (not just the British Isles) and the first African slaves arrived in 1619. With the Declaration of Independence in the next century the country began to move away from its British origins.

This trend was accentuated in the following century when in the mass migration 1840 and 1920 some 30 million flocked to America, the largest proportion from Ireland, Germany, Italy and the Austro-Hungarian Empire.

'For three centuries America was a frontier of Europe to which malcontents and adventure-seekers, people without opportunities or those with ambitions, could repair, if they could find the means and brave the journey and the transplantation', writes Charlotte Erickson.[3] The frontier spirit is an essential part of the American outlook.

Another aspect is the drive to success. 'They believe in the future as if it were a religion', writes Frances Fitzgerald.[4] 'They believe that there is nothing they cannot accomplish, that solutions wait somewhere for all problems, like brides.'

In this century the ethnic diversity has been increased still further by a considerable influx of non-Europeans from Latin America and Asia, lowering the proportion of people who can claim British or Irish descent still more. So the United States has a foreign feel — particularly as you move away from the Atlantic coastline. However, the foreignness is partly offset by the fact that Americans speak our language — or we speak theirs.

Foreign, yet familiar. American programmes figure prominently in British and European television schedules and American films dominate our cinema screens. However, we should be wary of taking every Hollywood product we see at face value. The American media are unsurpassed at creating myths, but prospective migrants need to get to grips with the reality of the place.

THE REGIONS OF AMERICA

Mention the United States and people think of Los Angeles, New York, Washington DC and Florida, since these are the places which regularly attract media attention and visitors from this side of the Atlantic. They also boast large expatriate communities — business people (New York), diplomats (Washington DC), film stars and other professionals (Los Angeles) sunseekers and retirees (Florida).

Yet these places are merely on the periphery. The United States is a large subcontinent almost twice the size of Europe and with even greater climatic and geographical diversity. New York does not convey an accurate picture of what the whole country is like any more than London can count itself representative of Germany, Spain or Albania. Before choosing where to put down roots, a detailed reconnaissance is advised.

The United States is a federal country of 255 million people where much of the day-to-day administration is in the hands of the individual states, and their representatives can offer you more information on opportunities than agencies of the Federal Government in Washington DC. It covers an area of 3.6 million square miles (9.4m sq km). In order to make the country more understandable we can break it down into regions.

New England

Connecticut (CT): *area:* 4,872 sq. miles; *pop.:* 3.3 million; *capital:* Hartford

Massachusetts (MA): *area:* 7,824 sq. miles; *pop.:* 6 million; *capital:* Boston

Maine (ME): *area:* 30,995 sq. miles; *pop.:* 1.2 million *capital:* Augusta

New Hampshire (NH): *area:* 8.993 sq. miles; *pop.:* 1.1 million; *capital:* Concord

Rhode Island (RI): *area:* 1,055 sq. miles; *pop.:* 1 million; *capital:* Providence

Vermont (VT): *area:* 9,273 sq. miles; *pop.:* 570,000; *capital:* Montpelier

This area preserves its strong traditional Puritan English outlook and boasts some of the country's leading academic institutions.

The Mid Atlantic Region

District of Columbia (DC): *area:* 63 sq. miles; *pop.:* 638,000;

Delaware (DE): *area:* 1,932 sq. miles; *pop.:* 700,000; *capital:* Dover

Maryland (MD): *area:* 9,837 sq. miles; *pop.:* 5 million; *capital:* Annapolis

New Jersey (NJ): *area:* 7,468 sq. miles; *pop.:* 7.8 million; *capital:* Trenton

New York (NY):*area:* 47,377 sq. miles; *pop.:* 18 million; *capital:* Albany

Pennsylvania (PA): *area:* 44,888 sq. miles; *pop.:* 12 million; *capital:* Harrisburg

Virginia (VA): *area:* 39,704 sq. miles; *pop.:* 6.4 million; *capital:* Richmond

West Virginia (WV): *area:* 24,119 sq. miles; *pop.:* 2 million; *capital:* Charleston

Perhaps the most important region as far as business and industry is concerned. Many major US companies have their headquarters here and many foreign companies choose to base their representatives here.

The South

Alabama (AL): *area:* 50,767 sq. miles; *pop.:* 4.1 million; *capital:* Montgomery

Arkansas (AR): *area:* 52,078 sq. miles; *pop.:* 2.4 million; *capital:* Little Rock

Florida (FL): area: 54,153 sq. miles; *pop,:* 13.5 million; *capital:* Tallahassee

Georgia (GA): *area:* 58,056 sq. miles; *pop.:* 6.7 million; *Capital:* Atlanta

Kentucky (KY): *area:* 39,669 sq. miles; *pop.:* 3.7 million; *capital:* Frankfort

Louisiana (LA): *area:* 44,521 sq. miles; *pop.:* 4.2 million; *capital:* Baton Rouge

Mississippi (MS): *area:* 47,233 sq. miles; *pop.:* 2.5 million; *capital:* Jackson

North Carolina (NC): *area:* 48,843 sq. miles; *pop.:* 6.8 million; *capital:* Raleigh

South Carolina (SC): *area:* 30,302 sq. miles; *pop.:* 3.6 million; *capital:* Columbia

Tennessee (TN): *area:* 41,155 sq. miles; *pop.:* 5 million; *capital:* Nashville

Not a popular place with immigrants, except for subtropical Florida which has attracted plenty of people from Britain, Latin America (especially Cuba) and Asia.

The Midwest
Illinois (IL): *area:* 55,645 sq. miles; *pop.:* 11.4 million; *capital:* Springfield
Indiana (IN): *area:* 35,932 sq. miles; *pop:* 5.7 million; *capital:* Indianapolis
Michigan (MI): *area:* 56,954 sq. miles; *pop.:* 9.3 million; *capital:* Lansing
Missouri (MO): *area:* 68,945 sq. miles; *pop.:* 5.2 million; *capital:* Jefferson City
Ohio (OH): *area:* 41,004 sq. miles; *pop.:* 11 million; *capital:* Columbus
Wisconsin (WI): *area:* 54,426 sq. miles; *pop.:* 5 million; *capital:* Madison

The hub of this vast area is Chicago, the nation's third largest city. However the mining and industrial sectors have been badly hit by the recession.

The Great Plains
Iowa (IA): *area:* 55,965 sq. miles; *pop.:* 2.9 million; *capital:* Des Moines
Kansas (KS): *area:* 81,778 sq. miles; *pop.:* 2.5 million; *capital:* Topeka
Minnesota (MN): *area:* 79,548 sq. miles; *pop.:* 4.5 million; *capital:* St Paul
Nebraska (NE): *area:* 76,644 sq. miles; *pop.:* 1.6 million; *capital:* Lincoln
North Dakota (ND): *area:* 69,300 sq. miles; *pop.:* 650,000; *capital:* Bismarck
South Dakota (SD): *area:* 75,952 sq. miles; *pop.:* 700,000; *capital:* Pierre

The great agricultural centre of the United States is in decline. On the credit side all six states reached the top ten in a quality of life ranking study in 1989. North Dakota came first.

The Rocky Mountain states
Colorado (CO): *area:* 103,595 sq. miles; *pop.:* 3.5 million; *capital:* Denver
Idaho (ID): *area:* 82,412 sq. miles; *pop.:* 1 million; *capital:* Boise
Montana (MT): *area:* 145,388 sq. miles; *pop.:* 825,000; *capital:* Helena

Utah (UT): *area:* 82,073 sq. miles; *pop.:* 1.8 million; *capital:* Salt Lake City

Wyoming (WY): *area:* 96,989 sq. miles; *pop.:* 470,000; *capital:* Cheyenne

Colorado with its capital, Denver, is the fastest growing state of the union. Salt Lake City is also an important centre, especially if you are of the Mormon persuasion.

The South West
Arizona (AZ): *area:* 113,508 sq. miles; *pop.:* 3.8 million; *capital:* Phoenix
New Mexico (NM): *area:* 121,335 sq. miles; *pop.:* 1.6 million; *capital:* Santa Fe
Oklahoma (OK): *area:* 68,655 sq. miles; *pop.:* 3.2 million; *capital:* Oklahoma City
Texas (TX): *area:* 262,017 sq. miles; *pop.:* 17.6 million; *capital:* Austin

Texas along with other places in the Sunbelt has attracted a good many immigrants in recent years and although the economy has had its ups and downs, there seem to be plenty of opportunities at the moment. Houston especially is an important centre.

The West
Alaska (AK): *area:* 570,833 sq. miles; *pop.:* 590,000; *capital:* Juneau
California (CA): *area:* 156,299 sq. miles; *pop.:* 31 million; *capital:* Sacramento
Nevada (NV): *area:* 109,894; *pop.:* 1.4 million; *capital:* Carson City
Oregon (OR): *area:* 96,184 sq. miles; *pop.:* 3 million; *capital:* Salem
Washington (WA): *area:* 66,511 sq. miles; *pop.:* 5.1 million; *capital:* Olympia

The Californian economy outranks most countries in size and has drawn migrants from all over the world. Its spectacular expansion, however, has been halted by the recession and the drop in demand for aircraft and defence-related equipment. Alaska stands apart from the rest of the West; mining and oil are the mainstay of its economy and it has much of the old frontier atmosphere.

The Islands
Hawaii (HI) and various US Pacific and Caribbean territories (including Puerto Rico, Guam, American Samoa, Virgin Islands)

Hawaii (HI): *area:* 6,425 sq. miles; *pop.:* 1.1 million; *capital:* Honolulu

While these places may be pleasant enough to live in employment opportunities tend to be restricted.

IMMIGRATION PROSPECTS

The USA's open-door policy on immigration came to an end in 1921 when the first Quota Act was passed. New legislation has been introduced to regulate the immigrant flow from time to time, the most recent being the Immigration Law of 1990 (IMMACT 1990).

Even so, 675,000 people will be admitted as immigrants in 1995, and this figure does not include returning residents and people entering on non-immigrant visas. Yet of this number around 70 per cent of the places are for family sponsored immigrants: 465,000 until 1995; 480,000 after 1995.

If you do not have family members in the US you will need to obtain a residence visa on the basis of your employment or entrepreneurial skills. The number of places allocated for this category is 140,000 and inevitably the distinguished and well-qualified get priority over the others. In any year the number of unskilled workers admitted will be at most 10,000.

Some 10,000 places are reserved for investors who create employment for at least ten other people. The actual amount required varies from area to area, but is unlikely to be under $500,000.

A new 'green card lottery' has come into effect in 1994 under which applicants from certain countries who fulfil the minimum requirements (a high school diploma or its equivalent) are selected at random. (Ireland and the UK are excluded this time round.) 55,000 places are envisaged under this scheme, but as vast numbers of applications are likely to be filed from all over the world and from within the US itself, the chances are pretty remote of gaining a green card — The Alien's Registration Receipt Card, to give it its proper name.

You should bear in mind that a large proportion of people who go to work in the United States do so on non-immigrant (temporary) work visas. These are reckoned to be less difficult to acquire than immigrant (permanent) visas, and are an option worth exploring.

The drawback with non-immigrant visas is that they normally require that you have an approved offer of employment. They are, however, renewable, and once you become established you might consider applying to the Immigration and Naturalisation Service (INS) for residential status, if you can qualify. For more about this see below, pp.165-72.

IMMIGRATION CHECKLIST

Full immigrant status can be granted on the basis of:

- family relationships (1–2)
- your trade or profession (employment based preferences)
- other criteria.

Work through the following questionnaire to assess your eligibility.

1. Do you have close relations who are citizens of the United States?

    YES   Go to 2
    NO   Go to 4.

2. Are you the spouse or child of a United States citizen? *or*
    Are you the parents of United States citizens who are 21 years old or more?

    YES   Your are an *immediate relative* and numerical limits do not apply. You should therefore experience no difficulty in getting an immigrant visa. But see section on Prohibited Immigrants.
    NO   Go to 3.

3. (a)   Arc you the unmarried son or daughter of a United States citizen? *or*
    (b)   Are you the spouse or child of a permanent resident? *or*
    (c)   Are you the unmarried son or daughter of a permanent resident and over 21? *or*
    (d)   Are you the married son or daughter of a US citizen? *or*
    (e)   Are you the brother or sister of a citizen aged 21 years or over? *or*
    (f)   Are you the spouse or child of a legalised alien?

    YES   You qualify for residence under the *Family Sponsored Preference* programme. However, you have to stand in the queue to take up places that have not been taken up by immediate relatives, and yo .. wait may last years rather than months.
        The annual numerical limit is determined by subtracting the

previous year's immediate relative total from the specific world-wide level of family sponsored immigrants (i.e. 465,000 or 480,000).

Note that there are various Family Sponsored Preference categories:

(a)   You come under FSP 1 where there is a quota of 23,400.
(b)   You come under FSP 2A for which there is a minimum quota of 87,394.
(c)   You come under FSP 2B for which there is a minimum quota of 26,266.
(d)   You come under FSP 3 for which there is a quota for 23,400.
(e)   You come under FSP4 for which there is a quota of 65,000 a year.

NO   You may be able to enter the country on the strength of your employment or entrepreneurial skills. Under the 1990 Immigration Act the number of employment based preference immigrants was increased substantially from 54,000 to 140,000. Go to 4.

4.   Are you an individual with extraordinary ability in the arts, sciences, education, business or athletics? (This has to be the Immigration and Naturalisation Service's opinion, not your own!) *or*

Are you a professor or researcher recognised internationally as outstanding in your field and with three years' experience entering the United States for a tenured or tenure track position? *or*

Are you a multinational executive or manager employed with the sponsoring employer or affiliate for at least one year in the three years preceding your application for residence or entry to the United States?

YES   You are regarded as a *priority worker* and fall into Employment-Based Preference Category One for which the annual quota is 40,000. No labour certification approval is required.
NO   Go to 5.

5.   Do you possess advanced qualifications in a professional field? *or*
Are you a person of exceptional ability in the arts, sciences or business?

YES   You could be considered for Employment-Based Preference Category 2 — *members of the professions* — for which the quota is 40,000 plus any unused visas from Category One. While it is not necessary to have worked for the same company for a year before entry to the country, labour certification is required. This means that employers need to obtain a certificate from the Department of Labor in their state demonstrating that there are no United States workers who are able, willing, qualified and available to take up the position for which they are seeking to recruit an alien.

NO   Go to 6.

6.   Are you a skilled worker with a minimum of two years' training or experience *or*

Are you a professional with a bachelor's degree? *or*
Is there a shortage of workers in your trade in the United States?

YES   You fall into Employment-Based Preference Category 3 — *professionals, skilled and unskilled workers*, for which the quota is 40,000 plus any unused visas from Categories One and Two. However no more than 10,000 visas are available to Unskilled Workers. Labour Certification is required (see above).

NO   Go to 7.

7.   Are you a minister of religion or religious worker?
Are you an overseas employee of the United States government?
Are you an employee of certain international organisations?
Are you a current or former employee of the United States government?

YES   You fall into Employment-Based Preference Category 4 — *special immigrants*— which also includes Panama Canal employees and others. The quota is 10,000.

NO   Go to 8.

8.   Are you an investor in a new commercial enterprise that will create full-time employment for at least 10 persons who are not members of your immediate family?

YES   For Employment Based Preference Category Five there are 10,000 visas for Foreign Investors, of which not less than 3,000 are reserved for investors in designated rural or high unemployment areas. The minimum investment is normally $1 million or $500,000 in these designated areas. (See also E1 and E2 visas in section on Other Non-immigrant Visas.)

NO   Go to 9 or look at section on non-immigrant visas.

9.   Beginning in October 1994 a new category of Diversity Immigrant visa will come into effect under which applicants from certain countries will be selected in random order, but not countries such as the UK or Eire which benefited from previous 'green card' lotteries.
      Applicants will be required to have either a high-school education or at least two years' work experience in an occupation that requires two years' training or experience. Only one petition may be submitted each year and there will be a quota of 55,000.
      There is also a special visa category for refugees and asylum seekers.

PROHIBITED IMMIGRANTS

Even though people may appear to fulfil the eligibility criteria, they could be turned down because:

● they suffer from communicable diseases (e.g. tuberculosis)
● they have a dangerous physical or mental disorder
● they have committed serious criminal acts
● they are terrorists, subversives, members of a totalitarian party
● they are likely to become public charges in the United States
● they have used fraud or other illegal means to enter the United States.

   If you have been an exchange visitor on a J-1 visa in the past you may have to live outside the United States for two years before you can apply for certain visas.

HOW TO APPLY FOR AN IMMIGRANT VISA

1. The first step

● For a *family sponsored immigrant* visa, your relative should normally file a petition (Form I-130) with the local office of the Immigration and Naturalisation Service (INS) in the United States.

- For an employment based immigrant visa Form I-140 is required. *Members of the profession, professionals, skilled and unskilled workers* must have their petitions filed by their prospective employers. But first the Department of Labor must certify that there are no qualified workers available for the proposed job. *Priority workers* may petition on their own behalf with the INS in the United States.

- *Investors* should file a Form I-526 petition with the INS.

2. Preliminary application
In most cases the consulate will send you two forms: the Preliminary Questionnaire for Residence (OF-169) and the Biographic Data for Visa Purposes Form (OF-179).

3. Interview
Eventually you will be called for an interview and will have to submit an Application for Immigrant Visa and Alien Registration (Form 230). The consular officer will inform visa applicants of the documents required to support the application (e.g. passport, birth certificate, police certificates).

4. Medical examination
You will need to undergo a medical examination conducted by a doctor designated by a consular officer, for which a fee is payable.

5. Issue of a visa
Immigrant visas are issued in the chronological order in which the petitions were filed, and you should not rely on being issued with a visa very promptly. If you fall into a category which is oversubscribed there may be a waiting period of some years.

6. Arrival in the United States
On arrival the immigration authorities will stamp a temporary 'green card' stamp in your passport. Your alien registration receipt card will be sent to you in the post several months later. At some later stage if you decide to apply for naturalisation, you will need to contact the nearest office of the Immigration and Naturalisation Service.

NON-IMMIGRANT (TEMPORARY) VISAS

As mentioned earlier, it is also possible to enter the United States to work on a non-immigrant (temporary) visa, and you may well find this a better

PLEASE TYPE OR PRINT YOUR ANSWERS IN THE SPACE PROVIDED BELOW EACH ITEM

1. SURNAMES OR FAMILY NAMES (Exactly as in Passport)	DO NOT WRITE IN THIS SPACE
2. FIRST NAME AND MIDDLE NAME (Exactly as in Passport)	
3. OTHER NAMES (Maiden, Religious, Professional, Aliases)	

4. DATE OF BIRTH (Day, Month, Year)   8. PASSPORT NUMBER

5. PLACE OF BIRTH
City, Province   Country   DATE PASSPORT ISSUED (Day, Month, Year)

6. NATIONALITY   7. SEX ☐ Male ☐ Female   DATE PASSPORT EXPIRES (Day, Month, Year)

9. HOME ADDRESS (include apartment no., street, city, province and postal zone)

10. NAME AND STREET ADDRESS OF PRESENT EMPLOYER OR SCHOOL (Postal Box number unacceptable)

11. HOME TELEPHONE NO.   12. BUSINESS TELEPHONE NO.

13. COLOR OF HAIR   14. COLOR OF EYES   15. COMPLEXION

16. HEIGHT   17. MARKS OF IDENTIFICATION

18. MARITAL STATUS
☐ Married ☐ Single ☐ Widowed ☐ Divorced ☐ Separated
If married, give name and nationality of spouse

19. NAMES AND RELATIONSHIPS OF PERSONS TRAVELING WITH YOU
(NOTE: A separate application must be made for each visa traveler, regardless of age.)

20. HAVE YOU EVER APPLIED FOR A U.S. VISA BEFORE, WHETHER IMMIGRANT OR NON-IMMIGRANT?
☐ No ☐ Yes   Where? _____
When? _____ Type of Visa? _____
☐ Visa was issued   ☐ Visa was refused

21. HAS YOUR U.S. VISA EVER BEEN CANCELED?
☐ No ☐ Yes   Where? _____
When? _____ By Whom? _____

22. Bearers of visitors visas may generally not work or study in the U.S.
DO YOU INTEND TO WORK IN THE U.S.? ☐ No ☐ Yes
If YES, explain

23. DO YOU INTEND TO STUDY IN THE U.S.? ☐ No ☐ Yes
If YES, write name and address of school as it appears on form I-20.

24. PRESENT OCCUPATION (If retired state past occupation)

25. WHO WILL FURNISH FINANCIAL SUPPORT, INCLUDING TICKETS?

26. AT WHAT ADDRESS WILL YOU STAY IN THE USA?

27. WHAT IS THE PURPOSE OF YOUR TRIP?

28. WHEN DO YOU INTEND TO ARRIVE IN THE USA?

29. HOW LONG DO YOU PLAN TO STAY IN THE USA?

30. HAVE YOU EVER BEEN IN THE USA?
☐ No ☐ Yes   When? _____
For How long? _____

NONIMMIGRANT VISA APPLICATION

COMPLETE ALL QUESTIONS ON REVERSE OF FORM

OPTIONAL FORM 156 (Rev 4-91) PAGE 1   50156-106
Department of State

NSN 7540-00-139-0053

Fig. 23. US non-immigrant visa application form.

166

31. (a) HAVE YOU OR ANYONE ACTING FOR YOU EVER INDICATED TO A U.S. CONSULAR OR IMMIGRATION EMPLOYEE A DESIRE TO IMMIGRATE TO THE U.S.? (b) HAS ANYONE EVER FILED AN IMMIGRANT VISA PETITION ON YOUR BEHALF? (C) HAS LABOR CERTIFICATION FOR EMPLOYMENT IN THE U.S. EVER BEEN REQUESTED BY YOU OR ON YOUR BEHALF?

(a) ☐ No ☐ Yes   (b) ☐ No ☐ Yes   (c) ☐ No ☐ Yes

32. ARE ANY OF THE FOLLOWING IN THE U.S.? (If YES, circle appropriate relationship and indicate that person's status in the U.S., ie. studying, working, U.S. permanent resident, U.S. citizen, etc.)

HUSBAND/WIFE _____   FIANCE/FIANCEE _____   BROTHER/SISTER _____

FATHER/MOTHER _____   SON/DAUGHTER _____

33. PLEASE LIST THE COUNTRIES WHERE YOU HAVE LIVED FOR MORE THAN 6 MONTHS DURING THE PAST 5 YEARS. BEGIN WITH YOUR PRESENT RESIDENCE.

Countries	Cities	Approximate Dates

34. IMPORTANT: ALL APPLICANTS MUST READ AND CHECK THE APPROPRIATE BOX FOR EACH ITEM:

A visa may not be issued to persons who are within specific categories defined by law as inadmissible to the United States (except when a waiver is obtained in advance). Are any of the following applicable to you?

– Have you ever been afflicted with a communicable disease of public health significance, a dangerous physical or mental disorder, or been a drug abuser or addict? .... ☐ Yes ☐ No

– Have you ever been arrested or convicted for any offense or crime, even through subject of a pardon, amnesty, or other such legal action? .... ☐ Yes ☐ No

– Have you ever been a controlled substance (drug) trafficker, or a prostitute or procurer? .... ☐ Yes ☐ No

– Have you ever sought to obtain, or assist others to obtain a visa, entry into the U.S., or any U.S. immigration benefit by fraud or willful misrepresentation? .... ☐ Yes ☐ No

– Were you deported from the U.S.A. within the last 5 years? .... ☐ Yes ☐ No

– Do you seek to enter the United States to engage in export control violations, subversive or terrorist activities or any unlawful purpose? .... ☐ Yes ☐ No

– Have you ever ordered, incited, assisted, or otherwise participated in the persecution of any person because of race, religion, national origin, or political opinion under the control, direct or indirect, of the Nazi Government of Germany, or of the government of any area occupied by, or allied with, the Nazi Government of Germany, or have you ever participated in genocide?.......... ☐ Yes ☐ No

A YES answer does not automatically signify ineligibility for a visa, but if you answered YES to any of the above, or if you have any question in this regard, personal appearance at this office is recommended. If appearance is not possible at this time, attach a statement of facts in your case to this application.

35. I certify that I have read and understood all the questions set forth in this application and the answers I have furnished on this form are true and correct to the best of my knowledge and belief. I understand that any false or misleading statement may result in the permanent refusal of a visa or denial of entry into the United States. I understand that possession of a visa does not entitle the bearer to enter the United States of America upon arrival at port of entry if he or she is found inadmissable.

DATE OF APPLICATION _____

APPLICANT'S SIGNATURE _____

If this application has been prepared by a travel agency or another person on your behalf, the agent should indicate name and address of agency or person with appropriate signature of individual preparing form.

SIGNATURE OF PERSON PREPARING FORM _____
(If other than the applicant)

DO NOT WRITE IN THIS SPACE

37mm x 37mm

PHOTO

Glue or Staple
photo here

Optional Form 156 (Rev. 4-91) PAGE 2
Department of State

Fig. 23. Continued.

167

U.S. Department of Justice
Immigration and Naturalization Service

Application to Extend/Change Nonimmigrant Status

OMB #1115-0093

START HERE - Please Type or Print

Part 1. Information about you.

Family Name	Given Name	Middle Initial

Address - In Care of:

Street # and Name		Apt. #

City	State

Zip Code

Date of Birth (month/day/year)	Country of Birth

Social Security # (if any)	A# (if any)

Date of Last Arrival Into the U.S.	I-94#

Current Nonimmigrant Status	Expires on (month/day/year)

Part 2. Application Type.

(See instructions for fee.)

1. **I am applying for:** (check one)
   a. ☐ an extension of stay in my current status
   b. ☐ a change of status. The new status I am requesting is: _____

2. **Number of people included in this application:** (check one)
   a. ☐ I am the only applicant
   b. ☐ Members of my family are filing this application with me.
      The Total number of people included in this application is (complete the supplement for each co-applicant) _____

FOR INS USE ONLY

Returned

Receipt

Date _____
Date _____

Resubmitted

Date _____
Date _____

Reloc Sent

Date _____
Date _____

Reloc Rec'd

Date _____
Date _____

☐ Applicant Interviewed

Date _____

☐ *Extension Granted*
to (date): _____

☐ *Change of Status/Extension Granted*
New Class: _____ To (date): _____

Fig. 24. US extension/change of status form.

168

Part 3. Processing information.

1. I/We request that my/our current or requested status be extended until (month/day/year) _____

2. Is this application based on an extension or change of status already granted to your spouse, child or parent?
   ☐ No   ☐ Yes (receipt # _____)

3. Is this application being filed based on a separate petition or application to give your spouse, child or parent an extension or change of status?
   ☐ No   ☐ Yes, filed with this application   ☐ Yes, filed previously and pending with INS

4. If you answered yes to question 3, give the petitioner or applicant name: _____

   If the application is pending with INS, also give the following information

   Office filed at _____   Filed on _____ (date)

Part 4. Additional Information.

1. For applicant #1, provide passport information.
   Country of issuance _____   Valid to: (month/day/year) _____

2. Foreign address:
   Street # and Name _____   Apt# _____
   City or Town _____   State or Province _____
   Country _____   Zip or Postal Code _____

Form I-539 (Rev. 12-2-91)   *Continued on back.*

If denied:
☐ Still within period of stay
☐ V/D to: _____
☐ S/D to: _____
☐ Place under docket control

Remarks

Action Block

To Be Completed by Attorney or Representative, if any
☐ Fill in box if G-28 is attached to represent the applicant

VOLAG# _____

ATTY State License # _____

Fig. 24. Continued.

169

Part 4. Additional Information. (continued)

3. Answer the following questions. If you answer yes to any question, explain on separate paper.

	Yes	No
a. Are you, or any other person included in this application, an applicant for an immigrant visa or adjustment of status to permanent residence?		
b. Has an immigrant petition ever been filed for you, or for any other person included in this application?		
c. Have you, or any other person included in this application ever been arrested or convicted of any criminal offense since last entering the U.S.?		
d. Have you, or any other person included in this application done anything which violated the terms of the nonimmigrant status you now hold?		
e. Are you, or any other person included in this application, now in exclusion or deportation proceedings?		
f. Have you, or any other person included in this application, been employed in the U.S. since last admitted or granted an extension or change of status?		

If you answered YES to question 3f, give the following information on a separate paper: Name of person, name of employer, address of employer, weekly income, and whether specifically authorized by INS

If you answered NO to question 3f, fully describe how you are supporting yourself on a separate paper. Include the source and the amount and basis for any income

Part 5. Signature. Read the information on penalties in the instructions before completing this section. You must file this application while in the United States

I certify under penalty of perjury under the laws of the United States of America that this application, and the evidence submitted with it, is all true and correct. I authorize the release of any information from my records which the Immigration and Naturalization Service needs to determine eligibility for the benefit I am seeking.

Signature	Print your name	Date

Please Note: If you do not completely fill out this form, or fail to submit required documents listed in the instructions, you cannot be found eligible for the requested document and this application will have to be denied

Part 6. Signature of person preparing form if other than above. (Sign below)

I declare that I prepared this application at the request of the above person and it is based on all information of which I have knowledge.

Signature	Print Your Name	Date

Firm Name
and Address

(Please remember to enclose the mailing label with your application)

Fig. 24. Continued.

170

option, particularly if you are not certain that you want to live in the USA permanently. If you later wish to seek permanent residence it is permissible to change your visa status. A non-immigrant visa application form is shown in Fig. 23 and a change of status form is shown in Fig. 24.

There are different types of non-immigrant visas, many of which are based on a specific offer of employment.

Here is a summary of the relevant types of visa.

● H1B   For *people with specialist knowledge* with a degree, equivalent experience or a licence to practice, hired to fill a position requiring a graduate. The employer has to provide a Labour Condition Application. (maximum length of stay: six years.)

● H2B   For other employees required to fill an employer's temporary need who do not qualify for an H1B visa. Labour certification is required, which means the employer has to satisfy the Department of Labor in his particular state that he is not depriving an American resident of employment by offering a post to a foreign national. H2A visas are for temporary agricultural workers.

● E1   Treaty Trader and E2 Treaty Investor visas are available to citizens of countries such as the UK which have signed the appropriate treaty with the UK. The Trader (E1) must be involved in substantial trade between the US and his country. The Investor (E2) must make a 'substantial' investment in the US (which normally involves the establishment or purchase of a business). Qualifying employees of such traders or investors may also receive E1 or E2 visas. E visas permit a potentially indefinite stay in the US and are the closest non-immigrant category to permanent residence.

● L1   The intra-company transferee visa is for *managers, executives or personnel with specialised knowledge* employed by a US company having a parent, affiliate, branch or subsidiary overseas for which they worked in a similar position. (Maximum stay is currently 5 or 7 years.)

OTHER NON-IMMIGRANT VISAS

If you plan to stay in the USA on business or for pleasure for three months or less no visa is required for a national of the UK or several other countries, mostly in Europe. For a stay of more than three months a B1 (business), B2 (tourist) or B1/B2 (combined) visa must be applied for in advance.

F1 Foreign Student visas are for people undertaking a course of academic study. (For full-time students in vocational schools an M visa is required.)

H1A visas are for nurses.

J1 Exchange visitor visas are available for temporary vacation employment, au pairs and certain traineeships and are available through the sponsoring organisation. Other traineeships require an H3 visa.

O1 visas are for people with extraordinary ability in the sciences, arts, education, business and athletics or extraordinary achievement in film and TV production. O2 visas are available for supporting personnel.

P1 visas are for certain recognised athletes, entertainers and artists going to compete or perform in the US and for their support personnel.

R1 visas are for people in religious occupations.

There are no less than 53 different types of non-immigrant visa, and for a more detailed discussion of these you should refer to the book *Applying for a United States Visa. How to Get a Job in America* also deals with non-immigrant visas in some detail.

EDUCATION

The public system of education is highly decentralised and schools vary from state to state and from district to district. The difference between schools in inner cities and those in prosperous suburbs is much more marked than in the UK. The schools tend to be run along different lines from those in the UK and Ireland: creativity is encouraged while discipline may seem non-existent. Around 10 per cent of pupils attend private schools or parochial schools (run by a religious denomination).

To secure a good start on the jobs market a college education is becoming increasingly important. Tuition at state colleges is normally free to students within the state, but accommodation is not and grants are few and far between. To study at a private college — and several of the leading universities in the USA are private — can work out extremely expensive. The US–UK Educational Commission and various American International Schools in the UK are good sources of information.

SOCIAL SECURITY

People who are used to the National Health Service may get something of a shock when they get to the USA. Although you make social security payments, Medicare (the government health service) is limited to the over-65s and long-term disabled, and if you do not fall into this category you need to prepare yourself for hefty medical bills or else insure yourself and your dependants. However, reform is in the air.

Most employees are covered by company health insurance schemes, but these schemes do not always refund the full cost of treatment and may exclude items such as dental care, which means you need to take out supplementary insurance. The Health Insurance Association of the United States publishes a useful booklet entitled *The Consumer's Guide to Health Insurance*.

Employers pay into a government insurance programme which pays unemployment benefit to employees who are made redundant. The United Kingdom has a social security agreement with the United States, but this does not cover health care. The Federal Benefits Unit, c/o the US Embassy can provide you with further information.

TAXATION

Contrary to general belief America is not a low-tax country, and you must expect to pay state and local taxes in addition to federal income tax. In contrast to Europe the US tends to favour direct taxation (income tax) rather than indirect taxation (e.g. VAT).

On arrival you will need to register with the nearest branch of the Social Security Administration to obtain a *taxpayer identification number*. Federal income tax is complicated, and you can obtain various guides to tax *(Your Federal Income Tax* and *US Tax Guide for Aliens)* from the Internal Revenue Service c/o your nearest US Embassy or Consulate.

ACCOMMODATION

In some cities and states property is eminently affordable; but you must expect to pay up to three or four times as much for a property in San Francisco as you would in Florida. There can also be price variation within states.

Law and practice regarding house purchase differ from state to state, but Don and Pan Philpott's *Florida: The AIM Home Buyer's Guide* is a useful introduction. You should only deal with real-estate brokers who are licensed and should enlist the services of an attorney (solicitor) who is not acting for the vendor or closely associated with the broker. Be prepared to shop around for mortgages.

SALARIES

Liberal arts	$20,244	Nursing	$27,358
Social sciences	$21,310	Civil engineering	$27,707
Business admin.	$21,845	Physics	$28,777
Geology	$24,080	Computer science	$31,389
Mathematics	$24,968	Electrical engineering	$32,107
Chemistry	$25,938	Mechanical engineering	$32,256
Accounting	$27,051	Chemical engineering	$33,380

Fig. 25. Typical starting salaries for new graduates (Bureau of Labor Statistics, US Department of Labor).

HOUSING COSTS
See Figure 26.

JOB-FINDING
Job Service, equivalent to Job Centres in the UK, is operated by states in conjunction with the US Department of Labor and recruits for both blue-collar and white-collar posts.

Among the UK-based organisations that can provide information and assistance are International Jobsearch, LEADS and Walker and Walker. Overseas Employment Services and Overseas Consultants publish lists of employment agencies. See also *How to Get a Job in America* (How To Books).

MIGRATION CONSULTANTS
US Visa Consultants, Law Office Edward S. Gudeon, BCL Immigration Services. The United States Embassy can provide a list of UK based lawyers who are able to advise on immigration matters.

FURTHER INFORMATION
Going USA (Outbound Newspapers) is a monthly newspaper aimed at migrants and visitors.

The US–UK Education Commission can provide you with information on education, training and other related matters.

The American Chamber of Commerce has a useful reference library, as does the United States Information Service, but to use either establishment you will need to make a prior appointment.

Notes
[1] *The United States of America*, RB Mowatt (1938).
[2] *News Summaries*, AJ Toynbee (14 July 1954).
[3] Article by Charlotte Erickson in *The United States: A Companion to American Studies* (Methuen 1987).
[4] *Fire in the Lake*, France Fitzgerald (1972).

Regional House Price Trends

City	1989	1990	1992	City	1989	1990	1992
Akron, Oh.	$64,500	$67,700	$75,500	Los Angeles, Cal.	$214,800	$212,800	$218,000
Albuquerque, N.M.	83,000	84,500	86,700	Louisville, Ky.	58,400	60,800	69,700
Anaheim/Santa Ana. Cal.	241,700	242,400	235,100	Madison, Wis.	76,500	82,300	89,400
Atlanta, Ga.	84,400	86,400	85,800	Memphis, Tenn.	78,100	78,100	83,600
Baltimore, Md.	96,300	105,900	111,500	Miami/Hialeah, Fla.	86,900	89,300	97,300
Baton Rouge, La.	63,800	64,900	71,800	Milwaukee, Wis.	79,600	84,400	96,100
Birmingham, Ala.	78,500	80,800	89,500	Minneapolis/St. Paul, Minn.	87,200	88,700	94,800
Boston, Mass.	181,900	174,200	168,200	Mobile, Ala.	56,700	59,100	63,300
Bradenton, Fla.	68,100	69,600	80,400	Nashville/Davidson, Tenn.	79,900	81,800	89,000
Buffalo, N.Y.	72,500	77,200	79,700	New Haven, Conn.	163,400	153,300	142,400
Charleston, S.C.	74,500	76,200	82,000	New Orleans, La.	70,600	67,800	68,400
Chicago, Ill.	107,000	116,800	131,100	New York, N.Y.	183,200	174,900	169,300
Cincinnati, Oh.	75,800	79,800	87,500	Oklahoma City, Okla.	53,500	53,200	59,800
Cleveland, Oh.	75,200	80,600	88,100	Omaha, Neb.	60,600	63,000	67,400
Columbia, S.C.	73,900	77,100	85,100	Orlando, Fla.	79,800	62,800	86,200
Columbus, Oh.	77,900	81,600	90,300	Philadelphia, Pa.	103,900	108,700	119,800
Corpus Christi, Tex.	64,900	63,200	62,500	Phoenix, Ariz.	78,800	84,000	84,700
Dallas, Tex.	93,400	89,500	90,500	Pittsburgh, Pa.	65,800	70,100	74,800
Daytona Beach, Fla.	63,400	64,100	63,600	Portland, Ore.	70,100	79,500	92,300
Denver, Col.	85,500	86,400	91,300	Providence, R.I.	130,200	127,900	120,300
Des Moines, Ia.	57,500	60,500	71,200	Sacramento, Cal.	111,700	137,100	135,600
Detroit, Mich.	73,700	76,700	77,500	St.Louis, Mo.	76,900	75,700	81,600
El Paso, Tex.	63,100	63,600	65,900	Salt Lake City/Ogden, Ut.	69,400	69,400	73,000
Grand Rapids, Mich.	64,200	68,300	73,000	San Antonio, Tex.	64,200	63,600	68,000
Hartford, Conn.	165,900	157,300	141,500	San Diego, Cal.	181,900	183,600	182,700
Honolulu, Hi.	270,000	352,000	342,000	San Francisco, Cal.	260,600	259,300	243,900
Houston, Tex.	66,700	70,700	78,200	Seattle, Wash.	115,000	142,000	141,000
Indianapolis, Ind.	71,200	74,800	80,100	Spokane, Wash.	52,400	55,500	71,300
Jacksonville, Fla.	69,300	72,400	75,100	Syracuse, N.Y.	79,300	80,700	77,400
Kansas City, Mo.	71,600	74,100	76,100	Tampa, Fla.	71,900	71,400	70,100
Knoxville, Tenn.	71,100	75,400	78,300	Toledo, Oh.	60,800	62,800	74,000
Las Vegas, Nev.	85,700	93,000	101,400	Tulsa, Okla.	62,600	63,900	68,500
				Washington, D.C.	144,400	150,200	152,500

Fig. 26. USA regional house price trends.

The average prices of family homes (National Association of Realtors)

Earnings by Occupation and Sex

	Median weekly earnings ($)			
	1990 Men	1990 Women	1991 Men	1991 Women
Managerial and professional specialty	717	507	741	519
Executive, administrative, and managerial	722	484	737	495
Professional specialty	712	525	744	548
Technical, sales, and administrative support	494	329	498	351
Technicians and related support	561	426	564	442
Sales occupations	506	284	499	311
Administrative support, including clerical	438	332	456	349
Service occupations	317	231	320	243
Private household	(1)	161	(1)	164
Protective service	454	369	494	436
Service, except private household and protective	273	231	279	244
Precision production, craft, and repair	487	319	488	354
Mechanics and repairers	477	476	472	541
Construction trades	486	(1)	478	(1)
Other precision production, craft, and repair	503	295	517	320
Operators, fabricators, and laborers	379	262	391	275
Machine operators, assemblers, and inspectors	391	261	403	272
Transportation and material moving occupations	426	296	421	320
Handlers, equipment cleaners, helpers, and laborers	308	249	316	269
Farming, forestry, and fishing	262	214	269	220

(1) *Data not shown where base is less than 100,000*

Fig. 27. Median usual weekly earnings of full-time wage and salary workers (Bureau of Labor Statistics, US Department of Labor).

176

13
Europe and the Rest of the World

What affects men sharply about a foreign nation is not so much finding or not finding familiar things; it is rather not finding them in the familiar place. (G.K. Chesterton, *Generally Speaking*) [1]

So far this book has concentrated on the countries which have traditionally been the main destinations for emigrants from the British Isles and elsewhere. All are former colonies that have felt the need at some time or another to boost their populations in order to develop the potential of their economies, and all continue to attract migrants.

However, we should not overlook the fact that people from our islands go off to live in other countries as well — sometimes for a very long time, sometimes for ever. If this is not emigration, what other word can you use to describe it?

In fact, history is full of examples of British and Irish people who have taken up permanent residence abroad in locations as varied as Argentina and Zimbabwe. By no means all of them started off with the intention of settling: some were sent there by their employers or on government service, but as they developed closer ties with the country concerned they decided to stay on.

Even today you will occasionally find a former member of the Indian army who has stayed on into retirement on the sub-continent, or a former Colonial Office official who has decided to end his days in South East Asia. There are British businessmen in Hong Kong who have spent the best part of their working lives in the Crown Colony, and doctors who have practised in far-off lands for decades.

If you find a country that you like very much and where you can make a decent living, there is no reason why you should not make it your home. Initially the authorities may not agree to offer permanent residence, but as you demonstrate your worth, some may be prepared to reconsider. Marriage to a national of the country concerned can be a very convincing argument in your favour.

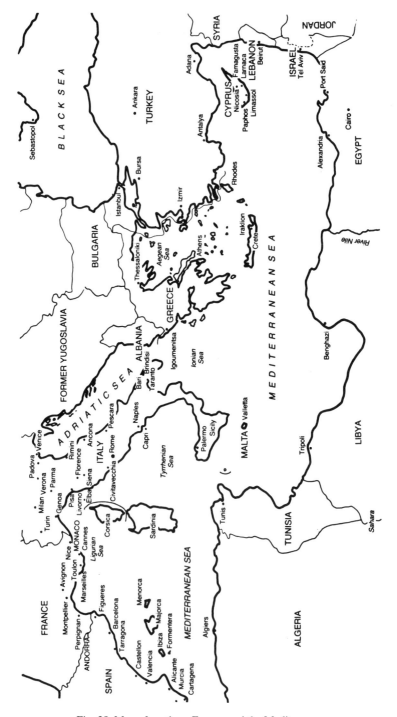

Fig. 28. Map of southern Europe and the Mediterranean

178

THE EUROPEAN UNION

One of the most popular areas for settlement these days is also the most accessible both geographically and administratively. Ironically, Europe which once used to be a net exporter of people has now become an area of the world that attracts migrants from other continents, and there is also movement of people between the countries themselves.

From the point of view of people living in the British Isles the countries of the European Union can be considered home ground these days. There is no need to obtain a special visa if you wish to take up employment anywhere in the Union, and there is no problem in transferring pension and social security rights.

The south of France and Italy have always been popular with people from Northern Europe, and in recent decades there has been an exodus to Portugal, Spain and other parts of France. It is a sign of the times that you can find in bookshops and libraries over a dozen books on living or buying a home in France.

A large number of British people live and work close to the hub of the European Commission in Brussels; and in most large centres you will find people from the British Isles working as company representatives, teachers, lawyers, accountants and in various other capacities. With the opening of the Channel Tunnel it will be feasible to live on one side of the English Channel and work on the other side.

Yet Europe presents a problem for some people. Despite their proximity to the British Isles the other EU countries are undeniably foreign. The people speak different languages from us, and if you cannot speak the language of the country you are living in, you will find yourself at a severe disadvantage. English may be the universal lingua franca, but it is not spoken universally in Europe.

Apart from the language problem, you may find that people on the European Continent behave differently and eat differently; their schools are different, and so are their laws and attitudes. 'Southern Europeans castigated by northerners for corruption in public life look with equal disapproval at the collapse of family values in the north', notes John Mole. 'They regard it as a duty to cheat the taxman and resent criticism by paragons of civic virtue who put their parents into old people's homes.' [2]

The English Channel represents a cultural divide which is far greater for many British people than the Atlantic Ocean. If you are attracted to Europe you first need to understand the people of the country you would like to live and work in and — above all — learn their language. If you go to live on the Continent without adequate preparation you may find it difficult to settle down.

OTHER EUROPEAN COUNTRIES

Language is not so much of a problem in places like Malta and Cyprus, which lie outside the European Union. While these countries have indigenous languages, past British influence means that most of the locals have an excellent command of English. Yet they also have well-educated populations and relatively few employment opportunities for outsiders, so you would need to make out a very good case for yourself in order to gain permanent entry.

Other countries, such as Austria and Switzerland, also have immigration controls, but there is a strong likelihood that they will be joining the European Union in the foreseeable future, and the situation may change. Turkey is another candidate for EU membership, but until an agreement is ratified you may find it difficult to enter on a permanent basis unless you have exceptional skills that are in great demand.

With the end of the Cold War some excellent opportunities are arising in Eastern Europe, as these countries seek to overhaul their outdated structures. It may be argued that many of these countries have economic problems and therefore little money to spend on foreign expertise. The spectre of instability looms in others, and the break-up of Yugoslavia may cause people to have second thoughts.

However, there is a brighter side. The European Union is currently providing a substantial amount of aid to the former Communist countries of Eastern Europe, and Britain itself is funding a range of projects with its Know-How Fund administered by the Foreign and Commonwealth Office. Some of these projects will have short lives; others may develop into long-term opportunities.

There are many people in the British Isles and elsewhere who have close ties with these countries. Their forbears may have fled these countries in recent decades, so they feel an affinity for a particular country and may have the added advantage of speaking the language. If you fall into this category and have the right skills, you could enjoy a bright future in certain parts of Eastern Europe.

THE MIDDLE EAST AND NORTH AFRICA

The Middle East, particularly the countries of the Arabian Peninsula, continues to offer plenty of opportunities for expatriates on contract. Some renew their contracts again and again, and spend years in a particular place, while others set up businesses, often with a local partner. The best prospects would seem to be in countries which have experienced British influence in the past (e.g. Oman, Qatar, Bahrain, the United Arab Emirates).

In order to enter any of these countries you normally need to have a definite offer of employment or to be a bona fide business person. Contract jobs are advertised in many of the overseas jobs papers; the construction, oil and gas, and education sectors lead the field. Many large firms employ representatives in the more prosperous countries of this area.

The Middle East is not regarded as the most stable part of the world, and expatriates living in Kuwait and Iraq have experienced considerable difficulties in recent years. While the region might be a good place to work in, it might be unwise to aim to become a permanent fixture.

AFRICA

In the past when Africa was a patchwork of colonies the continent was open to emigrants; it attracted large numbers of farmers, plantation owners and businessmen from Europe. Nowadays, the opportunities for permanent settlement are few and far between.

That is not to say that there are not opportunities for skilled people in Africa. Large numbers of people go out on aid programmes with voluntary and public agencies; missionary organisations continue to be strongly committed to Africa; there are jobs with construction companies, mining firms, oil companies and trading organisations; but for the most part these are contract posts. Often people will spend a period in these countries as part of a career progression in their firms.

Various countries in sub-Saharan Africa have suffered large-scale calamities in recent years including famine, drought, civil war and a serious AIDS epidemic, and many have experienced economic decline over the past decade. On the credit side, a few countries have managed to use their natural resources to their advantage and provide a better means of living for their people.

However, it has to be admitted that Africa faces an uncertain future and while investment is welcomed in some places, the current migration flow seems to be out of Africa rather than into it. Outside expertise is still needed, but governments do not usually offer permits of indefinite duration. By all means go to work there, but regard your permanent home as being elsewhere.

ASIA

Asia is a more complex continent than Africa. Certain parts of the continent have thriving economies which put those of the western world to shame. Several nations on the Pacific Rim, for instance, have long since shed their Third World status, and boast energetic and well-educated work forces. They no longer have to import expertise from outside.

Foreign firms, however, are welcome either as investors or traders, and there may be opportunities for you as an employee of such a firm or as a businessman or consultant in your own right. However, the chances of gaining a permanent residence visa are slight, unless you have a long-standing relationship with a particular country.

Hong Kong is an exception — for the time being. The Crown Colony boasts a very substantial British community, though its future after the territory reverts to China is uncertain. For the moment, however, the country has a very dynamic economy and is able to make good use of people with the right skills.

THE CARIBBEAN

Former British territories in this area may offer a few opportunities to investors, particularly people involved in tourism, but otherwise there are few opportunities for permanent settlement.

It may be easier to gain permanent residence visas for dependent territories, such as the Cayman Islands or Turks and Caicos Islands, but these have small populations and cover small areas.

LATIN AMERICA

This is a part of the world that deserves consideration, but you really need to be conversant in Spanish (Portuguese in the case of Brazil) before taking the plunge.

Argentina, for instance, has attracted immigrants from a wide range of countries in the past, and boasts a Welsh-speaking community in Patagonia. Other places worth considering are Chile and Uruguay, being stable countries with reasonable economic prospects.

Although not strictly speaking part of Latin America, the Falkland Islands are worth a mention here. The colony seems keen to attract settlers, and would doubtless appeal to those who want to 'get away from it all'.

[1] G.K. Chesterton, *Generally Speaking* (1928).

[2] John Mole, *Mind Your Manners* (Nicholas Brealey Publishing, 1992.)

14
Alternatives to Emigration

The survival of mankind will depend to a large extent on the ability of people who think differently to work together. (Geert Hofstede, *Culture's Consequences*) [1]

Do you really want to emigrate? It may seem strange to pose this question at this late stage of the book. However, emigration is essentially a long-term commitment, and at this point you may have doubts as to whether this is the right course of action for yourself and your family.

If you are unfamiliar with the country you are keen to emigrate to or if you have no experience at all of living outside the British Isles, it is prudent to think long and hard before embarking on such an enterprise. The most successful emigrants are often streetwise, with experience of living in different countries and usually with some prior knowledge of their destination.

Of course, no move is irrevocable. If things do not work out as you hoped, you do not have to stay — always assuming you have not run out of cash. You can move on elsewhere or you can move back to the UK. Even so, it is dispiriting if you have built up your hopes, and these are dashed after your arrival. All that effort, and all in vain.

However, you might consider an alternative strategy. Why not plan to stay in the country for just a short period — a few months perhaps, or even a year or two — and thus avoid uprooting yourself entirely? Then, if you do not like a place, you can move back to the UK in due course and resume your life where you left off.

STUDY ABROAD

This is an idea that may appeal especially to younger readers, including some who are still at school. It is excellent preparation for the global society in which we are now living.

School-age children

If you have relations or friends living abroad, they may be very happy to offer you hospitality and arrange with the local authorities for you to attend a local school. The Central Bureau for Educational Visits and Exchanges can provide further information about school exchanges and there are agencies which specialise in school and vacation placements, such as the ASSE International School Year Abroad Programme and the Experiment in International Living.

A term or a year abroad can be a useful educational experience, but it is important to investigate how it will fit in with examination commitments. Each of the countries featured in this book has an educational system which will differ to a greater or lesser extent from the British one. If GCSE or 'A' Level examinations are looming, you ought not to disrupt your course unduly by taking time out. In today's competitive world obtaining good results has to take precedence over worthwhile experiences.

An exception can be made in the case of an international school which prepares its pupils for the International Baccalaureate — an international qualification which is accepted by universities all over the world. United World Colleges in the United States and Australia are two of the schools which prepare young people for this qualification.

Further reading
Home from Home, Central Bureau, distr. Kuperard.

Students

Academic study is an international business these days and overseas universities welcome undergraduates from the British Isles and other countries. The snag is that you will have to pay fees to your alma mater and also have sufficient funds to cover your accommodation expenses. There are relatively few scholarships available at the undergraduate level which cover the whole period needed to obtain a first degree.

There may, however, be opportunities for you to make visits overseas as part of your course. If you are studying geology, for instance, the opportunity may occur for you to go and study the structure of Ayers Rock in Australia or the Grand Canyon in the United States; your educational institution or department may have an exchange scheme with a college overseas; and individual scholarships of short duration may be offered to promising students.

Further reading
Study Holidays, UNESCO.
Study Abroad, HMSO.
Teresa Tinsley, *How to Study Abroad*, How To Books.

WORK EXPERIENCE

School leavers
Once you have taken your school-leaving examinations you may feel that you wish to take time off before proceeding to further studies or starting your career in earnest. If you have contacts in overseas countries you may be able to make your own arrangements, and organisations such as the Central Bureau may be able to assist in the visa arrangements.

Otherwise, you could try specialist organizations, such as Gap Activities Projects and the Project Trust which can arrange for work placements such as working on a sheep farm in Australia or working as a tutor in a private school in New Zealand. However, demand for placements currently outstrips supply. Some religious organisations also organise exchanges.

Further reading
A Year Between, Central Bureau, distr. Kuperard.
Rosamund McDougall, *The Gap Year Guidebook,* Peridot Press.

Student exchanges
International experience is a highly prized attribute these days, and there are a number of organisations that cooperate with university and college departments to facilitate these. They include the AIESEC (management education), the International Association for the Exchange of Students for Technical Experience and the Central Bureau (hotel and catering management).

Most of these exchanges are aimed at graduates or undergraduates who are in their final year. Students of French, however, would be able to work as English assistants at schools in Quebec under a Central Bureau administered scheme. The same organisation may be able to advise on obtaining work visas if you manage to arrange your own exchange.

Working holidays
There are schemes, such as the British Australasia Educational Exchange, which enable students to undertake study-related work during the vacations. Other vacation work opportunities which are not necess-

arily study-related are provided by the British Universities North America Club (BUNAC) in Canada, the USA and Australia; and by Camp America.

Both Australia and New Zealand offer special work visas for young people enabling them to work for up to a year in these countries. There are certain restrictions of which you need to be aware (e.g. you must have a return air ticket and sufficient financial resources). The number of visas for New Zealand is limited.

Further reading
Summer Jobs Abroad, Vacation Work.
Working Holidays Central Bureau, distr. Kuperard.

Professional exchanges

Opportunities also exist for people who have already progressed in their careers. The League for the Exchange of Commonwealth Teachers organise exchanges of up to a year between British teachers and their counterparts in Australia, Canada and New Zealand; the Central Bureau organises exchanges with the United States.

A number of professional associations also organise exchanges for their members. They include the Royal College of Nursing and the International Agricultural Exchange Association. Increasingly international companies and companies with overseas affiliates are keen to transfer some of their key staff to other countries for short periods in order to broaden their experience.

CONTRACT WORK

Many of the people who go to work in other countries do so on a contract basis. There are certain advantages in this practice: the agency or employer arranges your visa, your travel expenses are normally paid and there may be other perks, such as subsidised accommodation.

Your contract is for a fixed period, which means that if the work environment has drawbacks you are not doomed to stay there forever. Many contracts can be extended by mutual agreement, and in some cases a contract job may eventually lead to a permanent position.

Even if it does not, you will be gaining valuable experience of working practices in the country and perhaps developing useful contacts. This experience and these contacts may well stand you in good stead if you decide to return to the country later in your career.

If you decide to stay on to work for some other organisation, you will need to check whether this is possible under the terms of your work visa. In the USA, for instance, a person's visa is tied to the job and either your new employer has to obtain approval (labor certification) to employ you or you have to apply for permanent resident status.

A number of agencies based in the UK specialise in recruiting for contract posts, for the United States in particular. There is a particular requirement for computer staff, medical staff and people in engineering disciplines. In the companion volume to this book, *How to Get a Job Abroad*, the subject of contract work is treated in much greater detail.

AN OVERSEAS POSTING WITH YOUR FIRM

If you join the armed services or the diplomatic service you will find yourself sent abroad whether you like it or not. Multinational firms are keen to breed international managers who feel as much at home in Albania as in Zanzibar. Is there any firm that would send you to the place you have set your heart on?

Not necessarily. If you are in a junior grade, you may well have to stay in the UK, though you may have the chance of an overseas posting as you progress upwards in the firm. Certain companies prefer to appoint nationals of the countries concerned to run their overseas subsidiaries; others expect their senior staff to be fully interchangeable.

If you are appointed to an overseas post, your employer will normally make all the visa arrangements for you, and you may have to renew your residence permit on a regular basis. If you become a permanent fixture, you may be able to convert to immigrant status. However, you cannot count on this, as each case is considered on its merit.

THE WORLD IS YOUR WORKPLACE

One day the notion of 'emigrating' may well sound dated — on a par with words like 'colonisation' and 'settler'. It is doubtful whether people will 'emigrate' in the twenty-first century; this will just be one of those expressions we come across in history books.

Until the middle of the present century people who went off to other countries usually stayed put. Only a minority — diplomats, members of the armed forces, senior businessmen — moved around from place to place. Nowadays we are more mobile: the jet age has changed our habits and our perspectives.

Moreover, the leading firms are now multinational and so are many of our emerging institutions — the European Community, the United Nations and its agencies. As a consequence staff (particularly senior staff) are more likely to be moved across national boundaries. Instead of pursuing their careers in their countries of origin they are having to get used to working in a global context.

This may sound an unnerving prospect to some older people, given the differences that exist between countries, but not to the younger generation who are already travelling more extensively than their parents ever dreamed of doing. This is not restlessness on their part — merely a sign of the times. We are starting to live in a world where all the barriers are down, where people with ambition need to function effectively anywhere in the world in no matter which country.

'International managers have it tough', observes Fons Trompenaars. 'They must operate on a number of different premises at any one time. These premises arise from their culture of origin, the culture in which they are working, and the culture of the organisation which employs them. [2] In such circumstances you cannot start too early to become a cosmopolitan.

Notes
[1] *Culture's Consequences*, Geert Hofstede (Sage, 1984).

[2] *Riding the Waves of Culture*, Fons Trompenaars (Economist Books, 1993).

Job Search Kit

POINTS TO REMEMBER WHEN SUBMITTING AN APPLICATION

● Make sure the information you provide is readily understandable to personnel staff and immigration officials in other countries. If you use acronyms such as BTEC, HND, FIPM, for instance, state what they actually mean and whether they are honorary titles or qualifications.

● Remember that certain countries and states have anti-discrimination laws, and you may need to suppress certain items of information — particularly with regard to race, religion, sex and age — in order to conform to local legislation. If you are applying to an employer or recruitment intermediary in the UK there is no need to be so circumspect.

● Correspondence posted abroad should be sent air mail and you should ensure that the envelope has an airmail sticker on it. In some cases you may find it more convenient — and certainly quicker — to fax information, and if you can give a fax number (of a friend or fax bureau) to which the recipient can reply, so much the better.

● All letters and CVs should be on A4-size paper and typed or word-processed.

Tel: 00 44 987 654321
Fax: 00 44 987 123456

2 Ivy Lane,
Little Chortling,
Salisbury SP81 6PY
UK

18th July 19...

Mr Ivor Shipley,
Kiwi Electronics Ltd,
Tonga Close,
Dunedin,
New Zealand

Dear Mr Shipley,

I note that you have recently been advertising in the *Dunedin Observer* for micro-processor engineers, and I would like to bring my qualifications and experience to your attention.

I have a B.Sc. in Electronics from Britannia University, Milton Keynes, and after working in the research department of Gadfly International in Birmingham for eighteen months I became assistant production engineer at Macclesfield Microprocessors in Cheshire, where I have worked for the last five years. During this time I have been responsible for designing and manufacturing microprocessors used in car components, refrigerators and defence equipment.

I am planning to emigrate to New Zealand in the near future and have been assured that there will be no difficulty in obtaining the necessary immigrant visa. I would therefore be glad to be considered for one of your vacancies.

Yours sincerely

John Bull

Fig. 29. Reply to a job advertisement.

Tel: 011 44 123 45678

39 Forth Street,
Edinburgh
Scotland EH2 9ZZ

30 January 19...

The Principal,
Dawson Academy,
Main Street,
Dawson City,
Yukon Territory,
Y5Q 9Z8
Canada

Dear Sir,

Having read a very interesting account about education in Canada in *The Times Educational Supplement*, I am writing to enquire whether you have any teaching vacancies at your establishment.

I am a graduate of the Inverness Teaching Institute and since leaving college I have taught general subjects to juniors at state schools in Arbroath, Scotland and Berwick on Tweed, England. I am currently teaching infants at a private school in Edinburgh, where I am also in charge of the school library.

I do not think there will be any difficulty in my obtaining a residence permit, since my fiancé is Canadian, and he has been offered a position with a major mining company based in the Yukon.

I shall be visiting relations in Vancouver at the end of March, and would be very pleased to call in to see you to discuss employment possibilities.

Please find enclosed photocopies of my certificates, my résumé and an international reply coupon for your answer.

Yours faithfully

Margaret MacGregor

Fig. 30. Speculative application letter.

191

Curriculum Vitae of
DEBORAH SCHWARZ

Address: 14 Ballymena Avenue, Cookstown, Co. Tyrone, Northern Ireland
Telephone: Cookstown (0111) 12345
Nationality: British

EDUCATION

1977–1984 Antrim High School
General Certificate of Education Ordinary Level: Art (C), Computer Science (B), English Language (B), French (C), Geography (A), Mathematics (C), Physics (A).
General Certificate of Education Advanced Level: Computer Science (B), French (B), Physics (C).

1984–1987   Liverpool University, UK
B Sc Hons   in Management and Computer Science (Class II A)

EMPLOYMENT RECORD

1984–1986   National Computer Bureau, Lancaster, UK:
            Research Assistant

1986–1989   McCready Computer Systems, Belfast, UK:
            Computer Programmer

1989–now   Sullivan Software Ltd
            Systems Analyst

Among the clients I worked with were Ballymena District Council, Parkinson Electronics and the Waverley Stores Group.

INTERESTS AND ACTIVITIES

Member of the Northern Ireland Ladies Golf Team.
Secretary of the Cookstown Branch of the Business & Professional Women's Association

OTHER DETAILS

Runner-up in the Northern Ireland Business Woman of the Year contest 1992
Member of the Institute of Management and British Computer Society
Fluent in French and Spanish
Holder of a full driving licence

Fig. 31. Curriculum Vitae (Résumé).

192

Profile of
MAXIMILIAN ROBERT LEE

Max Lee was born in Swansea and attended Fishguard High School where he was successful at six subjects at GCE Ordinary Level. He then studied at Camarthen Technical College for a Higher National Diploma (a post high school qualification) in Telecommunications. Four years later he obtained a City & Guilds certificate in Supervisory Management.

After qualifying in telecommunications he worked for the Post Office (now British Telecom) as a telecommunications engineer for ten years before moving to Tanzania where he was a telecommunications instructor at Dar es Salaam Polytechnic for three years under contract to the Overseas Development Administration (the British Government's aid agency).

On returning to England he joined Ogden Electronics as Overseas Sales manager with particular responsibility for Africa and Southern Europe. He negotiated a number of important contracts for the provision and installation of telecommunications equipment with the governments of Burundi, Chad, Lesotho and Andorra.

Ogden Electronics was taken over by its main rival last year and this resulted in large-scale redundancies among company employees, including Max Lee. Since parting company with the firm Max has taken a distance learning course in satellite communication techniques at the Open College and obtained a certificate in management from the Institute of Management.

Max Lee is a person with wide interests. He plays the trombone in the Bridgenorth Town Band, and is honorary treasurer of a local football club. He is a member of Portcawl Rotary Club and is well known in the area for his fundraising efforts for local charities.

He is now looking for a position overseas with a progressive firm that is able to make full use of his qualifications and experience in the field of telecommunications or management. He has spoken to immigration officials from your country and they believe he stands a good chance of obtaining a work permit if offered a job in your company.

Fig. 32. Alternative to a CV.

193

HOW SHOULD YOU BEHAVE AT AN INTERVIEW?

Do
● Be early, *never* late.

● Dress as you would for an office, even if the job involves wearing overalls, a uniform or other job-specific clothing.
● Be ready to show your education and training certificates.

● Talk about your qualifications, experience, and willingness to work.

● Show that you know about the company/organisation, what it is and does.

● Find out what might be expected of you, and when you will know if you are hired.

● Thank the interviewer when you leave.

Don't

● Don't smoke, discuss politics, tell jokes, criticise or 'put yourself down'.

● Don't talk about your family, problems or difficulties, unless you are asked.

● Don't take a friend or family member.

Don't forget

● Lying in an interview or on a résumé is grounds for being fired when the lie is discovered.

   (Adapted from a Canadian Immigration Fact Sheet on Employment)

Further Reading

GENERAL

Books

Allied Dunbar Expatriate Tax Guide (Longman Professional, annual).

The Au Pair and Nanny's Guide to Working Abroad, S. Griffith and S. Legg (Vacation Work Publications, 1989).

The British Expatriate's Financial Handbook (Directory Profiles, 148 Upper Richmond Road West, London SW14 8DP. Tel: (081) 392 2838. Fax: (081) 392 2817).

The CEPEC Recruitment Guide (Centre for Professional Employment Counselling, Kent House, 41 East Street, Bromley, Kent BR1 1QQ).

Contact Directory (Expat Network, International House, 500 Purley Way, Croydon CR0 4NZ. Tel: (081) 760 5100).

Culture's Consequences, Geert Hofstede (Sage, 1984).

The Directory (European Council of International Schools).

The Directory of Jobs and Careers Abroad, A. Lipinski (Vacation Work Publication, 1991).

The Gap Year Guidebook, Rosamund McDougall (Peridot Press, 2 Blenheim Crescent, London W11 1NN).

How to Find Temporary Work Abroad, Nick Vandome (How To Books, 1994).

How to Get a Job Abroad, Roger Jones (How To Books, 1991).

How to Retire Abroad, Roger Jones (How To Books, 1993).

How to Spend a Year Abroad, Nick Vandome (How To Books, 1992).

How to Study Abroad, Teresa Tinsley (How To Books, 1990).

International Benefits Guidelines William J. Mercer International, 4 Southampton Place, London WC1A 2DA).

International Directory of Executive Recruitment Consultants (Executive Grapevine, 4 Theobald Ct, Theobald St, Borehamwood, Herts WD6 4RN).

International Pay and Benefits Survey (PA Personnel Services, Hyde Park House, 60A Knightsbridge, London SW1X 7LE).

Mind Your Manners, John Mole (Nicholas Brealey Publishing, 1992).

Opportunities Overseas, Avril Harper (Grant Dawson, 1991).

The Overseas Property Buyer's Handbook, G. Pilgrem (David & Charles, 1991).

The Parent's Guide to Independent Schools (School Fees Insurance Agency).

Riding the Waves of Culture, Fons Trompenaars (Economist Books, 1993).

Study Holidays (UNESCO).

Summer Jobs Abroad (Vacation Work, 9 Park End Street, Oxford OX1 1HJ).

Sun, Sand and Cement: A Guide to Buying Overseas Property, Cheryl Taylor (Rosters, 1991).

The Traveller's Handbook, Sarah Gorman, ed. (WEXAS, 45 Brompton Road, London SW3 1DE, 1991).

Which School?, Gabbitas Truman & Thring (John Catt Ltd, Great Glenham, Saxmundham IP17 2DH).

Working Abroad: The Daily Telegraph Guide to Working Overseas, Geoffrey Golzen (Kogan Page, 1992).

Working Abroad: Essential Financial Advice for Expatriates and their Employers, Jonathan Golding (International Venture Handbooks, 1993).

Working Holidays (Central Bureau, distr. Kuperard).

Worldwide Personal Tax Guide (Ernst & Young International, 787 Seventh Ave, New York, NY 10019).

A Year Between (Central Bureau, distr. Kuperard).

Periodicals

BBC Worldwide (BBC World Service, PO Box 76, Bush House, Strand, London WC2B 4PH. Tel: (071) 240 3456).

The Economist (Economist Subscription Fulfilment Service, PO Box 14, Harold Hill, Romford RM3 8EQ. Tel: (04023) 81555. Fax: (04023) 81211).

The Expatriate (First Market Intelligence Ltd, 175 Vauxhall Bridge Road, London SW1V 1ER. Tel (071) 233 8593).

Expatriate Today (Directory Profiles Ltd, 148 Richmond Road West, London SW14 8DP. Tel: (081) 392 2838).

The Guardian Weekly (Guardian Publications Ltd, 164 Deansgate, Manchester M60 2RR. Tel: (061) 832 7200).

Home and Away (Expats International, 29 Lacon Road, East Dulwich, SE22 9HE. Tel: (081) 299 4986).

Jobfinder (Overseas Consultants, PO Box 152, Douglas, IOM).

London Calling (BBC World Service, PO Box 76, Bush House, Strand, London WC2B 4PH) (monthly programme bulletin).

Nexus (Expat Network, International House, 500 Purley Way, Croydon CR0 4NZ. Tel: (081) 760 5100).

Overseas Employment Newsletter (Overseas Employment Services, 1255 Laird Blvd, Town of Mount Royal, Quebec, H3P 2TI Canada).

Overseas Jobs Express (PO Box 22, Brighton, BN1 6HX. Tel: (0273) 440220).

Resident Abroad (Financial Times Magazines, Greystoke Place, Fetter Lane, London EC4A 1ND. Tel: (071) 405 6969).

The Weekly Telegraph (PO Box 14, Harold Hill, Romford, Essex RM3 8EQ. Tel: (0708) 381 000. Fax: (0708) 381211).

AUSTRALIA

Books

Australia Beyond the Dream Time, Thomas Keneally (BBC Books, 1987).

Australia Handbook (Promotion Australia — Australian Government Publishing Service).

Australia: A Handbook for Living and Working Down Under, Fiachra O'Marcaigh (Angus & Robertson, 1989).

The Australians: How They Live and Work, Nancy Learmonth (David & Charles, 1993).

The Book of Australia Almanac (Watermark Press, Sydney).

The Cost of Living and Housing Survey Book (Commonwealth Bank of Australia).

Culture Shock: Australia, Ilsa Sharp (Kuperard, 1992).

Directory of Australian Associations (Information Australia Group, 45, Flinders House, Melbourne, Vic 3000).

How to Get a Job in Australia, Nick Vandome (How To Books, 1992).

How to Live & Work in Australia, Laura Veltman (How To Books, 1992).

Job Guide for . . . . (State) (Australian Government Publishing Service).

Jobson's Mining Year Book (Dun & Bradstreet International).

Jobson's Year Book of Public Companies (Dun & Bradstreet International).

Kompass Australia (Peter Isaacson Publications).

Living in Australia: A Guide for New Settlers (Australian Govt Publishing Service, Canberra).

Long Stays in Australia, Maggie Driver (David & Charles, 1987).

Australia & NZ Employment Guide (Overseas Consultants, IOM).

Looking for a Job (Graduate Careers Council of Australia, PO Box 28, Parkerville, Vic).

Successful Migrating to Australia, Ian Gale (Macdonald/Queen Anne Press, 1990).

Periodicals

Australian News (Outbound Newpapers Ltd, 1 Commercial Road, Eastbourne BN21 3XQ. Tel: (0323) 412001. Fax: (0323) 649249).

Australian Outlook (Consyl Publishing Ltd, 3 Buckhurst Road, Bexhill on Sea TN40 1QF. Tel: (0424) 223111).

The Australian (70 Vauxhall Bridge Road, London SW1V 1RP.)

Australian Financial Review (12 Norwich Street, London EC4A 1BH. Tel: (071) 353 9321.)

The Melbourne Age (76 Shoe Lane, London EC4 3J0).

The Adelaide Advertiser (70 Vauxhall Bridge Road, London SW1V 2RP. Tel: (071) 834 9405.)

The Brisbane Courier Mail (Campbell Street, Bowen Hills, Brisbane 4006).

The Sydney Morning Herald (12 Norwich Street, London EC4A 1BH).

The West Australian (219 St George's Terrace, Perth, WA 6000).

Videos

Australia Yours (Eye View Video Productions, PO Box, Hitchin, Herts SG4 9UD).

Life in Australia (VH Productions, 8 Cedarhill Drive, Cannock, Staffs WS11 2NG. Tel: (0543) 577322).

CANADA

Books

The Blue Book of Canadian Business (Canadian Newspaper Services International, 65 Overlea Blvd, Suite 207, Toronto M4H 1P1.)

Canada Handbook (Statistics Canada, Ottawa).

Canadian Immigration Handbook, M.J. Bjarnason (International Venture Handbooks, 1994).

Corpus Almanac and Canada Sourcebook (Southam Information & Technology Group, Ontario).

Culture Shock: Canada, Robert Barlas and Pan Guek Cheng-Chen (Kuperard, 1992).

Directory of Canadian Employment Agencies (Overseas Consultants, IOM).

Canadian Key Business Directory (Dun & Bradstreet).

Live and Work in Canada, Avril Harper (Grant Dawson, 1992).
Living in Canada (Employment and Immigration Canada).
A Newcomer's Guide to Canada (Employment and Immigration Canada).

Periodicals
Canada News (Outbound Newspapers Ltd, 1 Commercial Road, Eastbourne BN21 3XQ. Tel: (0323) 412001. Fax: (0323) 649249).
Survey of Canadian House Prices (Royal LePage, 39 Winford Drive, Don Mills, ON M3C 3KC).
Toronto Globe and Mail (167 Temple Chambers, Temple Avenue, London EC4Y 0EA. Tel: (071) 936 2596. Fax: (071) 353 3343).
Vancouver Sun (8 Bouverie Street, 4th Floor, London EC4Y 8AX. Tel: (071) 583 7322).

NEW ZEALAND

Books
About New Zealand (Ministry of External Relations and Trade, Wellington).
Excellence: The New Zealand Education Directory (Ministry of Education).
How to Live and Work in New Zealand, Joy Muirhead (How To Books, 1994).
New Zealand: A Guide for New Settlers, G. Green (Immigration Division, New Zealand Department of Labour, 1988). A useful introduction, if you can get hold of a copy, but somewhat out of date.
The New Zealand Business Who's Who (Fourth Estate Holdings Ltd).
The New Zealand Immigration Handbook (Graphic Consultants Ltd in association with Malcolm Consultants).
The New Zealand Official Yearbook (NZ Department of Statistics).
New Zealanders: How They Live and Work, R.J. Johnston (David & Charles, 1976). Somewhat outdated.

Periodicals
The Dominion (PO Box 1297, Wellington).
The Evening Post (PO Box 1297, Wellington; 107 Fleet Street, EC 4A 2AN).
New Zealand Herald (PO Box 32, Auckland; 107 Fleet Street, London EC4A 2AN).
New Zealand News UK (PO Box 10, Berwick on Tweed, TD15 1BW. Tel: (0289) 306677. Also 25 Royal Opera Arcade, Haymarket, London SW1Y 4UY. Tel: (071) 930 6451) (weekly).

New Zealand Outlook (Consyl Publishing Ltd, 3 Buckhurst Road, Bexhill on Sea TN40 1QF. Tel: (0424) 223111) (bi-monthly newspaper for migrants).
Otago Daily Times (PO Box 181, Dunedin).
The Press (Private Bag, Christchurch).

Video
New Zealand on Video (NZ Promotions, PO Box 12, Auckland).

SOUTH AFRICA

Culture Shock: South Africa, D. Rissik (Kuperard/Times Editions, 1993).
Directory of Scientific and Technical Societies in South Africa (South African Council for Scientific and Industrial Research).
Education and Careers in Southern Africa (Erudita Publications, PO Box 25111, 2048 Ferreirasdorp).
Mini-Atlas of Southern Africa (Department of Foreign Affairs, South Africa).
National Trade Index of South Africa (Intratex) (includes addresses of Chambers of Industries and Mines, Chambers of Commerce, Employers' Trade Associations, and so on).
Opportunities for Graduates in Southern Africa (MSL Publications, PO Box 52518, Saxonwold 2132).
South Africa's New World (Leadership Publications, PO Box 1138, Johannesburg 2000).
South Africa Travel Guide (SATOUR, 4 Alt Grove, London SW19 4DZ).

Periodicals
South Africa News (Outbound Newspapers, 1 Commercial Road, Eastbourne BN21 3XQ. Tel: (0323) 412001. Fax: (0323) 649249).
Southern Africa Business Intelligence (Financial Times Newsletters, 1 Southwark Bridge, London SE1 9HL).
South African Business Report (South African Embassy, Trafalgar Square, London WC2N 5DP.)

UNITED STATES

Books
Applying for a United States Visa, Richard Fleischer (International Venture Handbooks, 1993).

Coping with America, Peter Trudgill (Blackwell, 1985).

Culture Shock: USA, Esther Wanning (Kuperard/Times Editions, 1991).

Directory of US Subsidiaries of British Companies (British American Chamber of Commerce, New York).

Doing Business in the USA (Oyez Publishing).

The Economist Business Travel Guide: United States (Economist Publications).

The Handbook of Private Schools (Porter Sargent Publishers, 11 Beacon Street, Boston MA 02108).

How to Get a Job in America, Roger Jones (How To Books, 1994).

How to Live and Work in America, Steve Mills (How To Books, 1992).

Living and Working in the USA, David Hampshire (Survival Books, 21 Lower Hanger, Haslemere, Surrey GU27 1LU).

Long Stays in America, R.W. Hicks and F. Schultz (David & Charles, 1986).

Occupational Outlook Handbook (US Department of Labor).

VGM's Careers Encyclopedia, C.T. Norback, ed. (VGM Career Books, Lincolnswood, IL).

What Colour is Your Parachute?, R.N. Bolles (Ten Speed Press, Berkeley, CA, 1992).

The World Almanac and Book of Facts (Pharaoh Books, New York).

Periodicals

Going USA (Outbound Newspapers Ltd, 1 Commercial Road, Eastbourne BN21 3XQ. Tel: (0323) 412001. Fax: (0323) 649249).

Christian Science Monitor, 25–28 Buckingham Gate, London SW1E 6LD. Tel: (071) 630 8666).

Wall Street Journal (200 Liberty Street, New York, NY 10281) (has four regional editions).

For a selection of leading newspapers state by state, please consult *How to Get a Job in America*.

EUROPE

How to Get a Job in Europe, M. Hempshell (How To Books, 1992).

How to Live and Work in Belgium, Marvina Shilling (How To Books, 1991).

How to Live and Work in France, Nicole Prevost Logan (How To Books, 1993).

How to Live and Work in Germany, Nessa Loewenthal (How To Books, 1991).

How to Live and Work in Italy, Amanda Hinton (How To Books, 1993).

How to Live and Work in Portugal, Sue Tyson-Wood (How To Books, 1993).

How to Live and Work in Spain, Robert A.C. Richards (How To Books, 1992).

Live and Work in Belgium, the Netherlands and Luxembourg, A. de Vries (Vacation Work, 1992).

Live and Work in France, Mark Hempshell (Vacation Work, 1991).

Live and Work in Germany, V. Pybus (Vacation Work, 1992).

Live and Work in Germany, Mark Hempshell (Grant Dawson, 1991).

Live and Work in Italy, Victoria Pybus and Rachael Robinson (Vacation Work, 1992).

Living and Working in Europe, E. Cobbe and J. MacCarthaigh (Gill & Macmillan, 1992).

Living and Working in Switzerland, D. Hampshire (Survival Books, 1991).

Living in France, P. Holland (Robert Hale, 1990).

Living in Italy, K. Menzies (Robert Hale, 1991).

Living in Portugal, Susan Thackeray (Robert Hale, 1990).

Living in Spain, John Reay-Smith (Robert Hale, 1989).

Long Stays in Belgium and Luxembourg, J. Hazlewood (David & Charles, 1986).

Long Stays in France, R. Mazzawi and D. Philpott (David & Charles, 1990).

Long Stays in Germany J.A.S. Abecasis-Philips (David & Charles, 1990).

Long Stays in Spain, Peter Favey (David & Charles, 1991).

Setting up in Italy, Sebastian O'Kelly (Merehurst, 1990).

Setting up in Spain, David Hewson (Merehurst, 1990).

Working in the European Community, A.J. Raban (HMSO, 1991).

Working in France, Carol Pineau and Maureen Kelly (Franc Books, BP 29, 94301 Vincennes, France).

OTHER COUNTRIES

How to Live & Work in Hong Kong, Martin Bennett (How To Books, 1992).

How to Live & Work in Japan, Aaron Hoopes (How To Books, 1992).

How to Live and Work in Saudi Arabia, J. McGregor and M. Nydell (How To Books, 1992).

Live and Work in Central America, Avril Harper (Grant Dawson, 1991).

UK Directory

Please note that on 16th April 1995 all British area telephone codes will change, and the number 1 should be inserted after the initial 0. Some cities will receive new codes: Bristol 0117 9; Leeds 0113 2; Leicester 0116 2; Nottingham 0115 9; Sheffield 0114 2.

GENERAL

Animal Aunts, 45 Fairview Road, Headley Down, Hants GU35 3HQ. Tel: (0428) 712611. (Offers pet and house-minding service.)

Association of Temporary and Interim Executive Services, 36–38 Mortimer Street, London W1N 7RB. Tel: (071) 323 4300.

BBC World Service, PO Box 76, Bush House, Strand, London WC2B 4PH. Tel: (071) 240 7790. (Publishes the magazine *BBC Worldwide* and *London Calling*, a monthly bulletin of its TV and radio programmes transmitted throughout the world.)

CBI Employee Relocation Council, Centre Point, 103 New Oxford Street, London WC1A 1DV. Tel: (071) 379 7400. (Advises companies moving staff; publishes *Relocation News*.)

Centre for International Briefing, Farnham Castle, Surrey GU9 0AG. Tel: (0252) 721194.

Chingford Quarantine Kennels Ltd, 160 Chingford Mount Road, Chingford, London E4 9BS. Tel: (081) 529 0979. Fax: (081) 529 2563.

Christians Abroad, 1 Stockwell Green, London SW9 9HP. Tel: (071) 737 7811. (Advice and contacts for people moving abroad.)

City of London Reference Library, 1 Brewers' Hall Garden, London Wall, London EC2V 5BX. Tel: (071) 638 8215. Fax: (071) 260 1847.

Economist Subscription Fulfilment Service, PO Box 14, Harold Hill, Romford RM3 8EQ. Tel: (04023) 81555. Fax: (04023) 81211.

Employment Conditions Abroad, Anchor House, 15 Britten Street, London SW3 3TY. Tel: (071) 351 7151. (Briefings and country reports.)

Expat Network, International House, 500 Purley Way, Croydon CR0
4NZ. Tel: (081) 760 5100. Fax: (081) 760 0469. (Expatriate service
organisation publishing *Nexus*.)

Expats International, 29 Lacon Road, London SE22 9HE. Tel: (081) 299
2484. (Expatriate service organisation.)

Golden Arrow Shippers, Horsford Kennels, Lydbury North, Shropshire
SY7 8AY. Tel: (05888) 240. (Pet transportation experts.)

Good Book Guide, 24 Seward Street, London EC1V 3PS. Tel: (071) 490
0900. (Mail order book service.)

Guardian Publications Ltd, 164 Deansgate, Manchester M60 2RR. Tel:
(061) 832 7200. (Publishers of *The Guardian Weekly*.)

Homesitters Ltd, The Old Bakery, Western Road, Tring, Herts HP23 4BB.
Tel: (0422) 891188. (Caretaking service.)

Inside Tracks, 10 Hartswood Road, London W12 9NQ. Tel (081) 749
0748. (Brief destination profiles of a number of cities in the US and
elsewhere.)

ISPA (International Society for the Protection of Animals, 106 Jermyn
Street, London SW1Y 6EE. Tel: (071) 839 3066.

Institute of Freight Forwarders, Redfern House, Browells Lane, Feltham,
Middlesex. Tel: (081) 844 2266.

International Baccalaureate European Office, 18 Woburn Square, London
WC1H 0NS. Tel: (071) 637 1682.

Manor Car Storage, PO Box 28, Clavering, Saffron Walden, Essex CB11
4RA. Tel: (0799) 550021.

Medical Advisory Services for Travellers Abroad (MASTS), London
School of Hygiene and Tropical Medicine, Keppel Street, London
WC1E 7HT. Tel: (071) 631 4408 and (0891) 224100.

Moran Stahl and Boyer, 136 Bond Street, London W1. Tel: (071) 629
8222. (Relocation experts.)

Overseas Resettlement Secretary, Board for Social Responsibility,
Church House, Dean's Yard, London SW1P 2NZ. Tel: (071) 222 9011.
(Can arrange contacts at destination.)

Par Air Services, Warren Lane, Colchester, Essex CO3 5LN. Tel: (0206)
330332. (Pet shipping agents.)

Women's Corona Society, 35 Belgrave Square, London SW1X 8QB. Tel:
(071) 235 1230. (Briefings, country reports, escort service.)

EDUCATION

Dean Associates, 51 High Street, Emsworth, Hants PO10 7AN. Tel:
(0243) 378022.

ECIS (European Council for International Schools), 21 Lavant Street, Petersfield, Hants GU32 3EW. Tel: (0230) 68244. (Publishes a directory of international schools.)

Gabbitas Truman & Thring, Broughton House, 6–8 Sackville Street, London W1X 2BR. Tel: (071) 439 2071.

GJW Education and Guardianship Services, Southcote, Coreway, Sidmouth, Devon EX10 9SD. Tel: (0395) 515614. (Guardianship and escort services.)

Independent Schools Information Service, 56 Buckingham Gate, London SW1E 6AG. Tel: (071) 630 8793.

International Baccalaureate European Office, 18 Woburn Square, London WC1H 0NS. Tel: (071) 637 1682.

Mercers College, Ware, Herts SG12 9BU. Tel: (0920) 465926.

SFIA (School Fees Insurance Agency) Educational Trust Ltd, SFIA House, 15 Forlease Road, Maidenhead, Berks SL6 1JA. Tel: (0628) 34291. (Publishers of *The Parent's Guide to Independent Schools*.)

Worldwide Education Service, 35 Belgrave Square, London SW1X 8QB. Tel: (071) 235 2880.

FINANCIAL PLANNING

Brown Shipley Lomond Ltd, 84 Coombe Road, New Malden, Surrey KT3 4QS. Tel: (081) 949 8811.

Expat Tax Consultants, Churchfield House, North Drive, Hebburn, Tyne and Wear NE31 1ES. Tel: (091) 483 7805.

Expatriate Advisory Services PLC, 14 Gordon Road, West Bridgeford, Nottingham, NG2 5LN. Tel: (0602) 816572.

Wilfred T. Fry Ltd, Crescent House, Crescent Road, Worthing, Sussex BN11 1RN. Tel: (0903) 231545.

Institute of Chartered Accountants in England and Wales, PO Box 433, Chartered Accountants Hall, Moorgate Place, London EC2P 2BJ. Tel: (071) 628 7060. Fax: (071) 920 0547.

Institute of Chartered Accountants of Scotland, 27 Queen Street, Edinburgh EH2 1LA.

Offord Fenning & Associates, 36 East Stockwell Street, Colchester, Essex CO1 1ST. Tel: (0206) 761252. Fax: (0206) 761239.

Seatax Ltd, 100 East Iaith Gate, Doncaster DN1 1JA. Tel: (0302) 364673.

Select Contract Services Ltd, PO Box 295, St Helier, Jersey JE4 8TZ. Tel: (0534) 69179. Fax: (0534) 30057.

TSW Consultants Ltd, 66 New Bond Street, London W1Y 9DF. Tel: (071) 491 2535. Fax: (071) 409 1557.

UK Expatriates Professional Advisory Services Ltd, 84 Grange Road, Middlesborough TS1 2LS. Tel: (0642) 221211.

(A more extensive list of financial services is featured in *The British Expatriate's Financial Handbook* (Directory Profiles).)

GOVERNMENT DEPARTMENTS

Benefits Agency, Department of Social Security, Overseas Branch, Benton Park Road, Newcastle upon Tyne, NE98 1YX. Tel: (091) 225 7341.

British Overseas Trade Board (BOTB), Department of Trade and Industry, 1 Victoria Street, London SW1H 0ET. Tel: (071) 215 5000.

Department of Health Leaflets Unit, PO Box 21, Honeypot Lane, Stanmore, Middx HA7 1AY. Tel: (0800) 555777.

Department of Health & Social Services, Overseas Branch, Lindsay House, 8–14 Callender Street, Belfast BT1 5DP.

Inland Revenue Claims Branch (Foreign Division), Merton Road, Bootle L69 9BL.

Inland Revenue (Inspector of Foreign Dividends), 72 Maid Marian Way, Nottingham NG1 6AS. Tel: (0602) 242299.

Inland Revenue Public Departments (Foreign Section), Ty-Glas, Llanishen, Cardiff CF4 5WN. Tel: (0222) 753271.

Ministry of Agriculture, Fisheries and Food, Animal Health Division IC, Hook Rise South, Toworth, Surbiton, Surrey KT6 7NF. Tel: (081) 330 4411.

INSURANCE AND PENSIONS

BUPA International, Imperial House, 40–42 Queen's Road, Brighton BN1 3WU. Tel: (0273) 820517.

Company Pension Information Centre, 7 Old Park Lane, London W1Y 3LJ.

Europea IMG, Fivash House, 9 Denne Parade, Horsham RH12 1JD. Tel: (0403) 63860. (Medical insurance).

Exeter Friendly Society (formerly Exeter HAS), Beech Hill House, Walnut Gardens, Exeter EX4 4DG. Tel: (0392) 498063. (Health insurance.)

Expacare, Dukes Court, Woking, Surrey GU21 5XB. Tel: (0483) 740090.

Hall-Godwins (Overseas) Consulting Co., Briarcliff House, Kingsmead,

Farnborough, Hants GU14 7TE. Tel: (0252) 5217071. (Pensions).

Healthsearch Ltd, 9 Newland Street, Rugby CV22 7BJ. Tel: (0788) 541855. (Impartial advice on healthcare plans.)

International Health Insurance Danmark A/S, Palaegarde 8, DK-1261 Copenhagen K, Denmark. Tel: (010 45) 3315 3099. Fax: (010 45) 3332 2560.

International Private Healthcare Ltd, PO Box 488, IPH House, Borehamwood, Herts WD6 4AN. Tel: (081) 905 2888.

Occupational Pension Advisory Service, 11 Belgrave Road, London SW1V 1RB. Tel: (071) 233 8080.

Private Patients Plan, Crescent Road, Tunbridge Wells TN1 2PL. Tel (0892) 512345. (Medical insurance.)

Society of Pensions Consultants, Ludgate House, Ludgate Circus, London EC4A 2AB.

Transcare International Ltd, 193–195 High Street, Acton, London W3 9DD. Tel (081) 993 6151. (Medical insurance.)

MIGRATION SERVICES

Australian Immigration Services, 38 Camden Road, Bexley, Kent DA5 3NX. Tel: (0322) 524686 (Australia).

BCL Immigration Services, Acorn House, 74–94 Cherry Orchard Road, Croydon CR0 6BA. Tel: (081) 6980 9621 and (081) 681 8339. Fax: (081) 667 0378 (Canada, USA, Australia).

Carriere Hall & Associates, 500 Chesham House, 150 Regent Street, London W1R 5FA. Tel: (071) 439 6288 (Canada).

The Hartford Consultancy, PO Box 328, Colchester, Essex CO1 1AA. Tel: (0206) 549406 (Australia).

Law Office Edward S. Gudeon, 17 Bulstrode Street, London W1M 5FQ. Tel: (071) 486 0813. Fax: (071) 224 2337 (USA).

Malcolm Consultants, 1 Hay Hill, London W1X 7LE. (071) 267 3575 (New Zealand).

Mallinick Ress Richman & Closeberg, 4 Carlton Gardens, London SW1Y 5AA. Tel: (071) 930 8702. Fax: (071) 930 8737 (South Africa).

Network Migration Services, Oxford House, College Court, Commercial Road, Swindon SN11 1PZ. Tel: (0793) 612222 (branches throughout UK) (New Zealand).

Ranfurly Johnston Mackey, 40 Bow Lane, London EC4M 9DT. Tel: (071) 489 8827 (New Zealand).

Sperry & Associates, 80 Worple Road, Wimbledon, London SW19 4HZ. Tel: (081) 947 5598 (New Zealand).

US Visa Consultants, 27 York Street, London W1H 1PY. Tel: (071) 224 3629. Fax: (071) 224 3859 (USA).

OTHER CONSULTANTS

International Jobsearch, 5 College Street, St Albans, Herts AL3 4PW. Tel: (0727) 865533. Fax: (0727) 846751.

Leeson's Employment, Accommodation and Data Services (LEADS), 4 Cranley Road, Ilford IG2 6AG. Tel: (081) 518 2603.

Walker & Walker Emigration, 24 Church Street, Kirby in Ashfield, Nottingham NG17 8LE. Tel: (0623) 753240. (Publish *Emigration Packs.*)

REMOVAL FIRMS

The following firms are bonded with the British Association of Removers (Overseas), 3 Churchill Court, 58 Station Road, North Harrow HA2 7SA:

Aberdeen (Grampian)   Clark & Rose Ltd. Tel: (0224) 782800.

Abingdon (Oxon)   Robinsons International Removals Ltd. Tel: (0235) 524992.

Aylesbury (Bucks)   Baxters (Removals) Ltd. Tel: (0296) 393335.

Bedford (Beds)   Harrison & Rowley. Tel: (0234) 272272.

Belfast (N. Ireland)   Thomas Johnson & Sons Ltd. Tel: (0232) 654241. John Morgan & Sons Ltd. Tel: (0232) 732333.

Berkhamsted (Herts)   S. Dell & Sons Ltd. Tel: (0442) 863959.

Billingham (Cleveland)   K. W. Devereux & Sons. Tel: (0642) 560854.

Birmingham (West Midlands)   Robinsons International Removals Ltd. Tel: (021) 449 4731.

Cardiff (S. Glamorgan)   Henry Chapman & Sons (Removals) Ltd. Tel: (0222) 492063.

Carlisle (Cumbria)   Binning Van Services Ltd. Tel: (0228) 20809.

County Down (N. Ireland)   McGimpsey Brothers. Tel: (0247) 888200.

Douglas (Isle of Man)   A. E. Corkill (Removals) Ltd. Tel: (0624) 75495/74631.

Edinburgh (Lothian)   Chariot Freight Services Ltd. Tel: (0506) 416377.

Edinburgh (Lothian)   Grampian Removers Ltd (trading as Chariots Freight Services). Tel: (0506) 416377.

Enfield (Middx)   Oceanair (International Removals) Ltd. Tel: (081) 805 1221.

Exeter (Devon)   Blatchpack Ltd. Tel: (0392) 61721.

Gateshead (T & W)   Hoults Removals Ltd. Tel: (091) 265 3696.

Glasgow (W. Scotland)   Hoults Removals Ltd. Tel: (041) 554 2101.
Kilmarnock Removals International. Tel: (0563) 20001.
Scotpac International Limited. Tel: (041) 776 5194.

Guildford (Surrey)   Kellys International Ltd. Tel: (0483) 60101.

Harrow (N. W. London)   Jim Candy Ltd. Tel: (081) 427 2659.

Hull (Humberside)   Selles (Removals & Storage) Ltd. Tel: (0482) 652528.

Lincoln (Lincolnshire)   Barnes of Lincoln. Tel: (0522) 537616.

Liverpool (Merseyside)   John Mason International Ltd. Tel: (051) 449 3938.

London E.   Double Overseas Removals Ltd. Tel: (081) 591 6929.
Geo. Copsey & Co Ltd. Tel: (081) 592 1003/6.
Harrow Green Removals Ltd. Tel: (081) 533 6000.
Scotpac International Ltd. Tel: (081) 591 3388.
Stewart Harvey & Woodbridge Ltd. Tel: (081) 517 0011.

London N.   Galleon International Shipping Co. Ltd. Tel: (081) 801 8833.
Michael Gerson Ltd. Tel: (081) 446 1300.
Hoults Removals Ltd. Tel: (081) 367 7600.
Pitt & Scott Ltd. Tel: (071) 607 7321.

London N. W.   Anglo Pacific International Ltd. Tel: (081) 965 1234.
Bollinger Ltd. Tel: (081) 961 1230.
Excess Baggage Co. Tel: (081) 965 3344.
Interdean Ltd. Tel: (081) 961 4141.
Davies Turner & Co Ltd. Tel: (051) 480 8118.

London (Kent)   DAP International Removals Ltd. Tel: (081) 310 3003

London (Middx)   Allied Pickfords. Tel: (081) 366 6521/5.
Leatherbarrows Removals & Storage Ltd. Tel: (081) 570 2241.
North American Van Lines. Tel: (081) 844 2000.

London (North)   Abels Ltd. Tel: (081) 449 4844.

London S. W.   Neale & Wilkinson Ltd. Tel: (071) 277 7410.
Bishops' Move London (Bishop & Sons Depositories Ltd). Tel: (071) 498 0300.
Davies Turner Worldwide Movers Ltd. Tel: (071) 622 4393.
GSI Normend Cargo Systems Ltd   Tel: (081) 208 2233.
Robinsons International Removals Ltd. Tel: (081) 452 5441/2.
Trans Euro Worldwide Movers (trading as Avalon Overseas Shipping). Tel: (081) 784 0100.

London S. E.   Alltransport Removals & Packing Ltd. Tel (081) 310 3311.

Finches of London Ltd. Tel: (081) 699 6766.

Manchester (Gt Manchester)   Frank Hill (R & S) Ltd. Tel: (061) 834 1317.

Interdean Ltd. Tel: (0612) 707 2016.

Middlesbrough (Cleveland)   E. Pearson & Sons (Teeside) Ltd. Tel: (0642) 247992.

Newhaven (Sussex)   The Old House (Removals & Warehousing) Ltd. Tel: (0323) 892934.

Northampton (Northants)   Walkers International Movers Ltd. Tel: (0604) 862111.

Norwich (Norfolk)   Richard Neave Ltd. Tel: (0953) 881348/

Nottingham   Transpakship. Tel: (0623) 441445.

Oxford (Oxon)   Cantay Group Ltd. Tel: (0865) 882989.

Luker Bros (Removals & Storage) Ltd. Tel: (0865) 62206/64653.

Preston (Lancs)   Stubbs International Movers Ltd. Tel:(0772) 52377.

Reading (Berkshire)   Robert Darvall Ltd. Tel: (0734) 864422.

Ferriday & Alder Ltd. Tel: (0734) 451030.

Rotherham (South Yorkshire)   H. Appleyard & Sons Ltd. Tel: (0709) 549718

Southampton (Hants)   Davies Turner & Co Ltd. Tel: (0703) 644733.

White & Co Plc. Tel: (0489) 783343.

Swansea (West Glamorgan)   Robbins of Swansea. Tel: (0792) 790101.

Taunton (Somerset) R. Crocker Removals. Tel: (0823) 259406.

Tonbridge (Kent)   F. Chapman & Sons Ltd. Tel: (089) 283 3313.

Warrington (Cheshire)   Roy Trevor Ltd. Tel: (0925) 30441/2.

Watford (Herts)   Amertrans. Tel: (081) 953 3636.

W. H. Humphreys & Son Ltd. Tel: (0923) 226206.

Weybridge (Surrey)   Luxfords of Weybridge. Tel: (0932) 842636.

Country Directory

AUSTRALIA

Addresses in the UK

Australian High Commission, Australia House, Strand, London WC2B 4LA. Tel: (071) 379 4334. Fax: (071) 240 5333. Visa Section Tel: (071) 438 8591. Visa information: (0891) 60333.

Consulates
Chatsworth House, Lever Street, Manchester. Tel: (061) 228 1344.
Hobart House, 80 Hanover Street, Edinburgh EH2 20L. Tel: (031) 226 6271.

Tourist office
4th Floor, Heathcoat House, 20 Savile Row, London W1X 1AF. Tel: (071) 434 4371.

Australian British Chamber of Commerce, Suite 615, 162–168 Regent Street, London W1R 5TB. Tel: (071) 439 0086. Fax: (071) 734 0872.
New South Wales Government Office, New South Wales House, 75 King William Street, London EC4. Tel: (071) 283 2166. Fax: (071) 522 0307.
Queensland Government Office, Queensland House, 392–393 Strand, London WC2R 0LZ. Tel: (071) 836 1333. Fax: (071) 240 7667.
South Australia Government Office, South Australia House, 50 Strand, London WC2N 5LW. Tel: (071) 930 7471. Fax: (071) 930 1660.
Victoria Government Office, Victoria House, Melbourne Place, Strand, London WC2B 4LJ. Tel: (071) 836 2656. Fax: (071) 240 6025.
Western Australia Government Office, Western Australia House, 115-116 Strand, London WC2R 4LC. Tel: (071) 240 2881. Fax: (071) 240 6637.
Centre for Australian Studies, 27–28 Russell Square, London WC1B 5DS. Tel: (071) 580 5876. Fax: (071) 255 2160.

The Hartford Consultancy, PO Box 328, Colchester, Essex CO1 1AA. Tel: (0206) 549406. (Visa application advice.)

Australian Immigration Services, 38 Camden Road, Bexley, Kent DA5 3NX. Tel: (0322) 524686. (Migration consultancy.)

Australian Club Card, 12 Ashton Cross, East Wellow, Romsey, Hants SO51 6AY. Tel: (0794) 23285. (Accommodation, car hire and meeting service.)

Visit Australia Ltd, Visit the World, 9 Marine Court, St Leonards on Sea, East Sussex TN38 0DX. Tel: (0424) 716544.

Commonwealth Bank of Australia, Financial & Migrant Information Service, 1 Kingsway, London WC2B 6DU. Tel: (071) 379 0955. Fax: (071) 836 0300.

R & I Bank of Western Australia Ltd, 85 London Wall, London EC2M 7AD. Tel: (071) 792 6351.

Westpac Banking Corporation, 75 King William Street, London EC4N 7HA. Tel: (071) 867 7000.

National Australia Bank Ltd, 6 –8 Token House Yard, London EC2R 7AJ. Tel: (071) 606 8070.

Australian Bookshop, 10 Woburn Walk, London WC1H 0JL. Tel: (071) 388 6080.

Addresses in Australia

British High Commission: Commonwealth Avenue, Canberra, ACT 2600. Tel: (062) 706666.

Consulates-General

Level 16, The Gateway, 1 Macquarie Place, Sydney, NSW 2000. Tel: (02 247) 7521.

17th Floor, 90 Collins Street, Melbourne, Vic 3000. Tel: (03 650) 4255. Fax: (03 650) 2990.

Prudential Building, 95 St George's Terrace, Perth, WA 6000. Tel: (09 322) 3200. Fax: (09 481) 4755.

BP House, 193 North Quay, Brisbane, Queensland 4000. Tel: (07 236) 2575. Fax: (07 221) 3009.

c/o Hassell Pty Ltd, 70 Hindmarsh Square, Adelaide, SA 5000. Tel (08 224) 0033.

Department of Immigration, Local Government and Ethnic Affairs, Benjamin Offices, Chan Street, Belconnen, ACT 2616.

Department of Social Security, Juliana House, Bowes Street, Phillip, ACT 2606.

Department of Employment, Education and Training, GPO Box 9880, Canberra,ACT 2601.

Australian British Trade Association, Commerce House, 26 Brisbane Avenue, Canberra ACT 2603.

Motor Vehicle Standards Administrator, Federal Office of Road Safety, GPO Box 1553, Canberra ACT 2601.

Commissioner of Taxation, GPO Box 2669, Canberra ACT 2601.

British Australian Pensioners Association, PO Box 35, Christie's Beach, South Australia 5165.

New South Wales Department of Education, GPO Box 33, Sydney 2001.

Office of Small Business, 139 Macquarie Street, Sydney 200.

Queensland Department of Education, PO Box 33, North Quay 4000.

Small Business Section, Dept of Commercial and Industrial Development, MIM building, 160 Ann Street, Brisbane 4000.

South Australia Education Department, GPO Box 1152, Adelaide 5001.

Small Business Advisory Bureau, 44 Pirie Street, Adelaide 5001.

Immigrant Promotion Unit, Department of Industry, Trade & Technology, 63 Pine Street, Adelaide 500.

Tasmania Education Department, GPO Box 169B, Hobart 7001.

Victoria Education Department, 2 Treasury Place, Melbourne 3002.

Small Business Development Corporation, 100 Exhibition Street, Melbourne 3000.

Western Australia Education Department, 151 Royal Street, East Perth 6000.

Small Business Advisory Service Ltd, 12 St. George's Terrace, Perth 6000.

Northern Territory Dept of Education, PO Box 4821, Darwin 5764.

Capital Schools Authority, PO Box 20, Civic Square, Canberra 2608.

A more comprehensive list of Australian addresses is included in *How to Live and Work in Australia.*

CANADA

Addresses in UK
Canadian High Commission, MacDonald House, 1 Grosvenor Square, London W1X 0AB. Tel: (071) 629 9492. Fax: (071) 491 3968.

Immigration Section, 38 Grosvenor Street, London W1X 0AA. Tel: (071) 258 6309. Fax: (071) 258 6506/6601.

National Tourist Office, Tel (071) 930 8540; (071) 258 6600.

Canada UK Chamber of Commerce, British Columbia House, 3 Regent Street, London SW1Y 4NZ. Tel: (071) 930 7711.

Agent General for Alberta, Alberta House, 1 Mount Street, W1Y 5AA. Tel: (071) 491 3430.

Agent General for British Columbia, British Columbia House, 1 Regent Street, SW1Y 4NS. Tel: (071) 930 6857.

Agent General for Quebec, Quebec House, 59 Pall Mall, SW1Y 5HJ. Tel: (071) 930 8314.

Agent General for Saskatchewan, Saskatchewan House, 16 Berkeley Street, W1X 5AE.

Canadian Imperial Bank of Commerce, Cottons Centre, Cottons Lane, London SW1 2QL. tel: (071) 234 6000.

Royal Bank of Canada, 71 Queen Victoria Street, London EC4V 4DE. Tel: (071) 489 1188.

Toronto Dominion Bank, Triton Court, 14/18 Finsbury Square, London EC2A 1DB.

Bank of Montreal, 11 Walbrook, London EC4. Tel: (071) 236 1010.

Bank of Nova Scotia, 10 Berkeley Square, London W1. Tel: (071) 491 4200.

Centre for Canadian Studies, University of Edinburgh, 21 George Street, Edinburgh RH8 9LD. Tel: (031) 667 1011.

Regional Canadian Study Centre, University of Leeds LS2 9JT.

Carriere Hall & Associates, 500 Chesham House, 150 Regent Street, London W1R 5FA. Tel: (071) 439 6288. (Immigration consultants.)

BCL Immigration Services, Acorn House, 74–94 Cherry Orchard Road, Croydon, Surrey CR0 6BA. Tel: (081) 680 9621. Fax: (081) 667 0378.

Addresses in Canada

British High Commission, 80 Elgin Street, Ottawa, Ontario K1P 5K7. Tel: Ottawa 237 1530.

British Consulates:

Suite 1910, College Park, 777 Bay Street, Toronto M5G 1G2. Tel: (416) 593 1290.

1155 University, Montreal H3B 3A7. Tel: (514) 866 5862.

10025 Jasper Avenue, Suite 1404, Edmonton T5J 1S6. Tel: (403) 426 0624.

Suite 800, 111 Melville Street, Vancouver V6E 3VB. Tel: (604) 683 4421.

Employment & Immigration Canada, 140 Promenade du Portage, Ottawa-Hull, PQ K1A 0C9. Tel: (819) 953 7449.

Health and Welfare Canada, Jeanne Mance Building, Tunney's Pasture, Ottawa, ON K1A 0K9.

Revenue Canada (Customs & Excise), Connaught Building, 555 Mackenzie Avenue, Ottawa, ON K1A 0L5.

Revenue Canada (Taxation), 875 Heron Road, Gloucester, ON K1A 0L8.

Technical Services Council, 10th Floor, 1 St Clair Avenue East, Toronto M4T 2V7 (Government recruitment agency).

Alberta Education, Devonian Building, 11160 Jasper Avenue, Edmonton T5K 0L2.

New Brunswick Department of Education, PO Box 6000, Fredericton E3B 5H1.

Newfoundland Department of Education, Confederation Building, PO Box 8700, St John's, NF A1B 4J6.

North Western Territories Department of Education, PO Box 1320, Yellowknife X1A 2C9.

Prince Edward Island Department of Education, PO Box 2000, Charlottetown C1A 7N8.

Canadian Association of Independent Schools, c/o Appleby College, Oakville, Ontario L6K 3PL.

Yukon Department of Education, PO Box 2703, Whitehorse Y1A 2C6.

Canadian Alliance of British Pensioners, 605 Royal York Road, Suite 202, Toronto, Ontario, Canada M8Y 4G5.

Royal LePage Real Estate Services, 39 Wynford Drive, Don Mills, ON M3C 3K5.

NEW ZEALAND

Addresses in the UK

New Zealand High Commission, New Zealand House, 80 Haymarket, London SW1Y 4TQ. Tel: (071) 930 8422. Fax: (071) 839 4580.

Immigration and visas
Tel: (071) 973 0366. Fax: (071) 973 0385.

Tourism
Tel: (071) 973 0360. Fax: (071) 839 4580.

Bank of New Zealand, 91 Gresham Street, London EC2V 7AX. Tel: (071) 973 0360. Fax: (071) 839 4580.

National Bank of New Zealand, 4th Floor, Abchurch Lane, London EC4N 7NB.

Malcolm Consultants, 1 Hay Hill, Berkeley Square, London W1X 7LF. Tel: (071) 267 3575. Fax: (071) 284 0080. Branches in Hong Kong and Taiwan. (Migration consultancy.)

Network Migration Ltd, Oxford House, College Court, Commercial Road, Swindon SN1 1PZ. Tel: (0793) 612222. Offices throughout UK. (Migration consultants.)

Ranfurly Johnston Mackey, 40 Bow Lane, London EC3M 9DT. Tel: (071) 489 8827. Fax: (071) 236 6325. (Human resource consultants.)

Sperry & Associates, 80 Worple Road, Wimbledon, London SW19 4HZ. Tel: (081) 947 5598. (Visa application preparation.)

Addresses in New Zealand

British High Commission, 44 Hill Street, Wellington 1.

British Consulate-General, 15th Floor, Faye Richwhite Building, 151 Queen Street, Auckland 1.

British Consulate, 173 Cashel Street, Christchurch 1.

British Trade Association, Commerce House, 126 Wakefield Street, Wellington.

British–New Zealand Trade Council, Level 3, 150 Willis Street, PO Box 3029, Wellington.

Department of Social Welfare, Private Bag 21, Wellington.

Department of Labour, Charles Fergusson Building, Box 3705, Auckland.

Inland Revenue Department, PO Box 2198, Wellington.

Customs Department, PO Box 2218, Wellington.

Ministry of Education, 45-47 Pipitea Street, Thorndon, Private Box 1666. Wellington.

Ministry of Transport, PO Box 2175, Wellington

New Zealand Association for Migration and Investment, PO Box 518, Tauranga. (A group of organisations which assist immigrants, including business migrants.)

New Zealand Chambers of Commerce, PO Box 11-043, Europa House, 109 Featherstone Street, Wellington.

Southern Cross Healthcare, Private Bag 99934, Newmarket, Auckland (Medical insurance).

Independent Schools Council, PO Box 52222, Wellington.

Harcourts Real Estate, PO Box 99549, Newmarket, Auckland.

Challenge Realty, PO Box 6, Hobson Street, Auckland.

The Professionals, 525 Manukau Road, Epsom, Auckland (estate agency).

Sheffield Consulting Group, PO Box 5621, Auckland (UK Office: Sheffield International, 14–18 Copthall Avenue, London EC2R 7DJ).

SOUTH AFRICA

Addresses in the UK

South African Embassy, Trafalgar Square, London WC2N 5DR. Tel:

(071) 930 4488. Fax: (071) 321 0834; Visa Section. Tel: (071) 839 2211.

South African Tourism Board, 5–6 Alt Grove, Wimbledon, London SW19. Tel: (081) 944 8080.

UK South Africa Trade Association, 45 Great Peter Street, London SW1P 3LT.

South African Airways, 251–259 Regent Street, London W1R 7AD. Tel: (071) 734 9841. (Branches in Manchester, Birmingham and Glasgow.)

SA Placements, 2 The Mill House, The Hill, Cranbrook, Kent TN17 3AH. Tel: (0580) 714184. Fax: (0580) 713054. (Management and recruitment consultants to South African industry who also arrange monthly briefings for would-be emigrants and jobseekers.)

Mallinick, Ress, Richman & Closenberg, 4 Carlton Gardens, Pall Mall, London SW1Y 5AA. Tel: (071) 930 8702. Fax: (071) 930 8737. (South African attorneys.)

International Travellers Service, 414 King's Road, London SW10. Tel: (071) 376 8679. Tax: (071) 376 4393. (Relocation specialists.)

First National Bank of Southern Africa, 4th Floor, 10 Foster Lane, London EC2V 6HH. Tel: (071) 606 7050.

Nedbank Ltd, 20 Abchurch Lane, London EC4N 7AD. Tel: (071) 623 1077.

Volkskas Bank, 52/54 Gracechurch Street, London EC3V 0EH. Tel: (071) 528 8296.

Pam Golding Properties International, 5th Floor, BNZ House, 91 Gresham Street, London EC2V 7BL. Tel: (071) 600 5420. Fax: (071) 726 8611. (Estate agents.)

Seef International Properties, Premier House, 112 Station Road, Edgware, Middx HA8 7BJ. TeL (081) 951 5656. Fax: (081) 954 9378. (Estate agents.)

Argus SA Newspapers Ltd, 32/33 Hatton Gardens, London EC1N 8DL. Tel: (071) 831 0882.

Stoke & Lindley-Jones Ltd, 26 Stone Hill House, Stone Hills, Welwyn Garden City, Herts AL8 6NA. Tel: (0707) 326688 (represents a number of South African trade and professional publications).

Addresses in South Africa

British Embassy, 255 Hill Street, Pretoria; 91 Parliament Street, Cape Town.

British Consulate-General, 19th Floor, Sanlam Centre, Cnr Jeppe and Von Wielligh Streets, PO Box 10101, Johannesburg 2000.

British Consulate, Southern Life Centre, 8 Riebeck Street, PO Box 500,

Cape Town 8000; and Fedlife House, 320 Smith Street, PO Box 1404, Durban 4001.

Ministry of National Health, Civitas Building, Struben Street, Private Bag X399, Pretoria 0001.

Cape Education Department, PO Box 13, Cape Town 8000.

Natal Education Department, Private Bag 9044, Pietermaritzburg 3200.

Orange Free State Education Department, PO Box 521, Bloemfontein 9300.

Transvaal Education Department, Private Bag X76, Pretoria 0001.

The Independent Schools Council, 31 St David Road, Houghton 2196.

The Catholic Institute of Education, PO Box 93230, Yeoville 2143.

The SA Board of Jewish Education, PO Box 46204, Orange Grove 2119.

British Retirement Pensioners Society (SA), PO Box 1641, Durban, South Africa 4000.

1820 Settlers Association of South Africa, 601 Norvic, 93 De Korte Street, Braamfontein, Johannesburg 2001. (UK representative: Outbound Newspapers.)

Association of Chambers of Commerce of South Africa, JCC House, PO Box 91267, Empire Road, Auckland Park, Johannesburg.

National Association of South African Architects, PO Box 7322, Johannesburg 2000.

South African Medical and Dental Council, PO Box 205, Pretoria 0001.

South African Nursing Council, PO Box 1123, Pretoria 0001.

Pharmaceutical Society of South Africa, Pharmacy House, PO Box 31360, Braamfontein 2018.

Division of Veterinary Services, Private Bag X138, Pretoria 0001.

UNITED STATES OF AMERICA

Addresses in the UK

United States Embassy: 24 Grosvenor Square, London W1A 2JB. Tel: (071) 499 9000. (Includes Customs Attaché, Federal Benefits Agency, Internal Revenue Service.)

Visa Branch, 5 Upper Grosvenor Street, London W1A 2JB. Tel: (071) 499 7010.

United States Information Service, 55/56 Upper Brook Street, London W1A 2JB.

United States Consulate: Queen's House, Queen Street, Belfast BT1 6EQ.

United States Tourist Office: PO Box 1EN, London W1A 1EN. Tel: (071) 439 7433.

US–UK Educational Commission, 62 Doughty Street, London WC1N 2LS. Tel: (071) 404 6994.

American Chamber of Commerce, 75 Brook Street, London W1Y 2EB.

British American Chamber of Commerce, 10 Lower John Street, London W1R 3PE. Tel: (071) 287 2676.

Office of the State of New York, 25 Haymarket, London SW1Y 4EN. Tel: (071) 839 5079.

Office of the State of California, 14 Curzon Street, London W1Y 7FH. Tel: (071) 629 8211.

US Visa Consultants, 27 York Street, London W1H 1PY. Tel: (071) 224 3629. Fax: (071) 224 3859 (immigration consultants).

Law Office Edward S Gudeon, 17 Bulstrode Street, London W1M 5FQ. Tel: (071) 486 0813. Fax: (071) 224 2337 (immigration lawyer).

BCL Immigration Services, Acorn House, 74–94 Cherry Orchard Road, Croydon, Surrey CR0 6BA. Tel: (081) 680 9621. Fax: (081) 667 0378 (immigration consultants).

Cahners Publishing Co, 27 Paul Street, London EC2A 4JU. Tel: (071) 618 7030 (a subsidiary of Reed-Elsevier which is the largest publisher of American trade and professional periodicals).

Addresses in the US

British Embassy: 3100 Massachussetts Ave NW, Washington, DC 20009. Tel: (202) 462 1340.

British consulates

California: Suite 312, 3701 Wiltshire Boulevard, Los Angeles, CA 90010. Tel: (213) 385 7381; 1 Sansome Street, Suite 850, San Francisco, CA 94101. Tel: (415) 981 3030.

Florida: Brickell Bay Office Tower, Suite 2110, 1001 S Bayshore Drive, Miami, FL 33131. Tel: (305) 374 1522.

Georgia: Suite 2700, Marquis One Tower, 245 Peach Tree Centre Avenue, Atlanta, GA 30303.

Illinois: British Consulate: 33 North Dearborn Street, Chicago, IL 60602. Tel: (312) 346 0810.

Massachussetts: Suite 4740, Prudential Tower, Prudential Centre, Boston MA 02199. Tel: (617) 437 7160.

New York: British Consulate: 845 Third Avenue, New York, NY 10022. Tel: (212) 593 2258.

Texas: 813 Stemmons Tower West, 2730 Stemmons Freeway, Dallas TX 75207. Tel: (214) 637 3600; Suite 2250, Dresser Tower, 601 Jefferson, Houston TX 77002. Tel: (713) 659 6270.

Washington State: 820 First Interstate Center, 999 Third Avenue, Seattle, WA 98104. Tel: (206) 622 9255.

British American Chamber of Commerce, 275 Madison Avenue, New York NY 10016-1128.

British American Chamber of Commerce, c/o Barclays Bank, 3150 California Street, San Francisco, CA 94115.

British Florida Chamber of Commerce, Suite 550, 2121 Ponce de Leon Blvd, Coral Gables, FL 33134.

Department of Health and Human Services, 200 Independence Ave SW, Washington DC 20201-0001.

Department of Labor, 200 Constitution Ave, NW, Washington DC 20210-0001.

American Automobile Association, 8111 Gatehouse Road, Falls Church VA 22042.

Health Insurance Association of America, 1025 Connecticut Avenue, NW, Washington DC 20036-3998.

US Small Business Administration, PO Box 1000, Fort Worth, TX 76119.

A more extensive list of addresses state by state can be found in *How to Get a Job in America* in this series.

Index

accommodation, 42, 85-87
Africa, 181
agents general, 34
alternatives, 183-188
application, 27-27
arrival, 65
Asia, 182

Australia, 93-110
  area, 93
  assessment, 26, 29
  Australian Capital Territory (ACT), 97
  banking, 87
  business skills test, 104-105
  Commonwealth Employment Service, 88
  concessional family visa, 100, 101
  conveyancing, 87
  description, 93-95
  designated areas, 25
  driving rules, 88
  education, 107
  healthcare, 107
  housing, 109
  immigration checklist, 99
  immigration process, 27
  independent entrant visa, 106
  job finding, 109
  map, 94
  New South Wales, 95
  non residence visas, 101
  Northern Territory, 97
  Queensland, 95-96
  points table, 102-103
  points test, 101
  'pool', 106
  population, 93
  prospects, 98
  qualifications, 25
  social security, 107
  South Australia, 96
  South Australia Migration Unit, 37, 89
  sponsorship, 106
  states, 95-96
  Tasmania, 96
  taxation, 92, 107
  Victoria, 96-97
  Western Australia, 97
  work practices, 92
balanced outlook, 53
banking, 66, 87
Benefits Agency (DSS), 78-79
book classification, 32
books, 31-32
bookshops, 32
briefing notes, 35, 61
briefing organisations, 66-67
British Airways, 75, 80
British Broadcasting Corporation (BBC), 90
British diplomatic missions, 63, 71, 91
Brown H, 65
business grants, 560
business prospects, 50-51
business visits, 63-64
buying a home, 87

Canada, 111-127
  Alberta, 115
  application process, 119
  assessment form, 120-121
  British Columbia, 113, 115
  business migration, 122
  Canada Employment Centres, 88
  description, 112-113
  designated occupations, 118, 119
  education, 123-125
  employment authorisation, 123
  entrepreneur, 122
  healthcare, 125
  history, 111
  housing, 124-126
  immigration policy, 117-118
  immigration procedures, 117, 119
  investor 122
  job finding, 126
  lifestyles, 116-117

Manitoba, 115
map, 111
multiculturalism, 111
New Brunswick, 114
Newfoundland, 113
North West Territories, 116
Nova Scotia, 113
Ontario, 114-115
pension, 125
points system, 118
Prince Edward Island, 114
priority occupations, 25
prospects, 117-119
Quebec, 111, 113, 114, 119
regions, 113-116
Saskatchewan, 115
self-employed, 112-123
social security, 125
temporary visas, 123
visas, 22
work practices, 93
Yukon, 116

cancelling deliveries, 68
car, 68-69
Caribbean, 182
Centre for International Briefing, 31, 67
chambers of commerce, 34-35
character, 26
children, 43, 69-70, 91
Chesterton G K, 177
choosing a country, 54-55
Christians Abroad, 35, 65
Church of England, 65-66
citizenship, 30
climate, 45, 46-49
clothes, 70-71
consulates, 34
contacts, 37-40, 59-60
contract work, 186-187
Cooke A, 54
cost of living, 42-43
cost of migration, 41-42, 57
criminals, 16
customs, 87
CVs, 192-193

Dickens, C., 15, 17
decison making, 54-56
Dean Associates, 70
De Kleerk, F.W., 141
dentist, 76
Department of Health, 75
determination, 53
doctor, 76

documentation, 27, 78
double taxation agreements, 83-83
driving licence, 71, 87-88

Eastern Europe, 180
economic development boards, 63-64
economy, 50, 62
education, 43, 69-70, 91
egalitarianism, 45
electoral registration, 71
emigration (definition), 15
emigration packs, 35
embassies, 34
employer, 27
employment agencies, 60, 88
Employment Conditions Abroad, 35, 67
employment legislation, 63
enterprise, 53
environment, 45
Erickson, C., 155
Europe, 177-180
European Commission, 179
European Union, 22, 50, 179-180, 188
exchanges, 185-186
Expat Network, 35
expatriate societies, 89

family, 43
financial advice, 71-72
first aid kit, 77
Fitzgeral, F., 155
friends, 37, 89

gap year, 185
Gale I, 31
global careers, 188
guardianship, 70

health, 74, 75-76, 89-90
high commissions, 34
highway code, 88
history of migration, 16-17
Hofstede, G., 183
Hollywood, 19
home in UK, 72-73
homesickness, 90
housing, 43
Hong Kong, 177
Huxley, E., 93

immigration consultants and lawyers, 27-
    30, 60-61, 63, 85
immigration fees, 41
immigration officials, 19, 27-29, 50-51
immigration policy 21-23

immigration procedures, 15
immigration quotas, 24
independent migrants, 28-29
Inland Revenue, 82-83
Inside Tracks, 35
inspection visits, 36-37, 62-63
insurance, 73-74
international managers, 188
investment, 74

Jerome, J.K., 57
job advertisements, 58-59, 88
job applications, 190-191
job finding, 57-64, 88-89
job search consultants, 60-61
job transfer, 61, 187
Johnston, R., 130

languages, 179
Latin America, 182
legal matters, 115
letting property, 73
libraries 31-32, 78
licences to practise, 25
life assurance, 74

mail, 72, 90
medical matters, 75-77
Mercers' College, 70
Micawber, 15, 17
Middle East, 180-181
migration consultants, 15-16, 27-30, 60-
    61, 85
migration seminars, 36
Ministry of Agriculture (MAFF), 79-80
'model' migrants, 19-20, 51-54
Mole, J., 179
Mowatt, R.B., 155

national insurance, 77
naturalisation, 30
networking, 59-60
newspapers, 33, 58-59

New Zealand, 128-139
    approved occupations, 25, 131, 132, 134
    area, 129
    assessment, 26, 132, 136-137
    cars, 138
    description, 129-30
    economy, 130
    education, 135-138
    family immigrants, 131
    general immigrants, 131-132, 133
    healthcare, 135
    history, 29

    housing, 138
    immigration checklist, 132-134
    immigration controls, 131
    immigration policy, 131-132
    job finding, 138
    map, 128
    non immigrant visas, 134-135
    North Island, 130-131
    points system, 136-137
    'pool', 132
    population, 129
    prospects, 131-132
    social security, 135
    South Island, 129, 132

Palmerston Lord, 31
Pascal, B., 85
passport, 77-78
pension, 78-79
periodicals, 33, 58-59
personal qualities, 18
pets, 79-80
pioneer, 53-54
points system, 24
political affiliations, 26
power of attorney, 80
preparation, 65-84
Pringle, J.D., 93
priority areas, 25
priority occupations, 25
private schools, 69-70
professional associations, 59, 88
prohibited immigrants, 26
prospects, 50
Proust, M., 41
'pull' factors, 18
'push' factors, 17

qualifications, 16, 25, 51-52

rainfall, 46-47
reasons for migrating, 17-19, 42
reconnaissance, 36-37, 62-63
recruitment consultants, 60
regional diversity, 54-55
registration, 91
relations, 21, 23-24, 27
removals, 80-82
renting a home, 86-87
resourcefulness, 52
Richler, M., 111

screening, 27-28
selectivity, 15
self-employment, 50-51
selling up, 72-73

settling in, 85-92
shopping list, 38-39
social security, 77 91

South Africa, 140-153
    area, 142
    banking, 149-150
    Cape Province, 143
    citizenship, 149
    conveyancing, 87, 150-151
    cost of living, 150
    customs duty, 150
    description, 142-143
    documentation, 148-149
    education, 151-152
    exchange control, 149-150
    financial matters, 149-150
    healthcare, 151
    history, 141-143
    housing, 150-151
    immigration questionnaire, 146-147
    immigration policy, 144-145
    immigration procedures, 145-149
    jobsearch, 152
    map, 140
    Natal, 143
    Orange Free State, 143
    people, 143-144
    political background, 143-144
    population, 142
    Settlers Association, 152-153
    social security, 151
    Transvaal, 143
    unemployment, 145

speculative job search, 59
standard of living, 42-43, 44
starting work, 91-92
state offices, 34
study abroad, 183-185
suitability, 51-54
support for immigrants, 89

tact, 52
taxation, 82-83, 91
temperature, 48-49
temporary work, 89
Thomas, R., 65
Toye, W., 111
Toynbee, A.J., 155
tourist boards, 34-35
tourist brochures, 34, 45
trade unions, 59
travel, 83
Trollope, A., 29
Trompenaars, F., 1888

twinning links, 59-60

unemployment benefit, 42

United States, 155-176
    area, 156
    conveyancing, 153
    education, 172
    employment based preference cate-
        cories, 162-163, 165
    family sponsored preference, 161-162,
        164
    Great Plains, 158
    history, 155-156
    healthcare, 172-173
    housing, 173, 176
    immediate relatives, 161
    immigration checklist, 161-164
    immigration policy, 160-161
    investors, 163-164
    Islands, 159-160
    map, 154
    Mid Atlantic Region, 157
    Mid West, 158
    New England, 156-157
    non immigrant visas, 165-172
    population, 156
    prohibited immigrants, 164
    prospects, 160-161
    regional diversity, 54
    regions, 156-160
    Rocky Mountain States, 158-159
    salaries, 174-175
    social security, 172-173
    South, 157-158
    South West, 159
    taxation, 173
    visa application procedure, 164-165
    visas, 22, 23
    work practices, 92

utilities, 68, 92

vaccination, 75
vehicle registration document, 68
vetting procedures, 27
visas, 21-23, 28, 77-78

Wilde, O., 93
will, 83
Women's Corona Society, 35, 67
work experience, 185
work practices, 92, 186
work prospects, 50
working holidays, 185-186
Worldwide Education Services, 70